I0153283

ELITE MARTIAL ARTISTS
WORLDWIDE

SECRETS TO LIFE
LEADERSHIP & BUSINESS

V O L U M E   I I I

GRANDMASTER JESSIE BOWEN
A N D   G L O B A L   M A R T I A L   A R T S   L E A D E R S

Elite
PUBLICATIONS

Elite Martial Artists Worldwide Volume III: Secrets to Life, Leadership & Business
by Grand Master Jessie Bowen

Published by:
Elite Publications
2120 E Firetower Rd. # 107-58
Greenville, NC 27858
Tel: 919-618-8075
info@elitepublications.org
Visit us online at: www.elitepublications.org

Copyright © 2025 Elite Publications
Cover & interior designed by Krystal Harvey, Tiger Shark, Inc.

FIRST PRINTING: MARCH 2025

LIBRARY OF CONGRESS CONTROL NO.: 2025903859

PAPERBACK ISBN-13: 978-1-958037-30-0

HARDCOVER ISBN-13: 978-1-958037-31-7

KINDLE & EBOOK ISBN-13: 978-1-958037-32-4

CONTENTS

INTRODUCTION
WELCOME TO ELITE MARTIAL ARTISTS WORLDWIDE
By Jessie Bowen.. 1

SECRETS TO
LIFE... **4**

CHAPTER 1
HOW MARTIAL ARTS PRINCIPLES CAN ENHANCE LEADERSHIP, BUSINESS & PERSONAL LIFE
By John Connelly...5

CHAPTER 2
THE RELATIONSHIPS THAT DEVELOPED A LEADER
By Ron Dargan.. 17

CHAPTER 3
THE MAGIC INGREDIENT TO HAVING A SUCCESSFUL LIFE
By Juanita Kapp..28

CHAPTER 4
INTENT INTO ACTION PART II
By Todd Norcross..39

CHAPTER 5
KEEPING A GROWTH MINDSET: THE KEY TO LIFELONG SUCCESS
By Jessica C. Phillips..49

CHAPTER 6
SECRETS TO LIFE: THE POWER OF THREE
By Rocci Twitchell.. 58

SECRETS TO
LEADERSHIP **63**

CHAPTER 7
CHOSEN TO LEAD
By Jessie Bowen... 64

CHAPTER 8
LEADERSHIP SECRETS
By James Debrow III.. 74

CHAPTER 9
THE SECRETS TO LEADERSHIP
By Linda Denley... 86

CHAPTER 10
THE GOLD STANDARD
By Al Farris... 94

CHAPTER 11
A GUIDE TO LEADERSHIP
By Thomas Fleming.. 101

CHAPTER 12
**MARTIAL ARTS: A FOUNDATION FOR LEADERSHIP &
LIFELONG ACHIEVEMENT**
By John Kerecz... 109

CHAPTER 13
**EXECUTIVE LEADERSHIP IN MARTIAL ARTS:
PRINCIPLES, CHALLENGES & STRATEGIES**
By Jean Kfoury... 118

CHAPTER 14
**THE INFLUENCE OF CONFIDENCE, DISCIPLINE &
RESPECT IN LEADERSHIP**
By Stephen Miller.. 129

CHAPTER 15
LEADERSHIP BY EXAMPLE
By Michael Sullenger.. 138

SECRETS TO
BUSINESS... 146

CHAPTER 16
THE SECRETS TO BUSINESS SUCCESS FROM A MARTIAL ARTS PERSPECTIVE
By Dennis Brown..147

CHAPTER 17
BUSINESS ASPECTS OF TAEKWONDO
By John Connelly...155

CHAPTER 18
COMMUNICATION
By Nick Donato.. 167

CHAPTER 19
KEVIN HOOKER'S JOURNEY IN MARTIAL ARTS & BUSINESS
By Kevin Hooker..176

CHAPTER 20
BUILDING A BUSINESS FROM THE GROUND UP
By Maggie Messina...185

CHAPTER 21
THE JOY OF LIVING BUSINESS: VISUALIZE & WIN
By Nathan Ray..193

INTRODUCTION

WELCOME TO ELITE MARTIAL ARTISTS WORLDWIDE VOL. III

BY JESSIE BOWEN

Martial arts is more than a self-defense practice; it is a way of life, a philosophy that extends beyond the dojo and into everyday living. Over the years, martial artists' discipline, resilience, and wisdom have shaped not only individuals but also communities, businesses, and leadership worldwide.

In our previous editions, *Elite Martial Artists in America: Secrets to Life, Leadership, and Business, Volumes I and II*, we gathered the insights of over fifty accomplished martial artists, each sharing their personal journeys, leadership strategies, and business acumen. These books provided a foundation for understanding how martial arts principles—discipline, respect, perseverance, and honor—translate into personal and professional success.

Now, *with Elite Martial Artists Worldwide: Secrets to Life, Leadership, and Business, Volume III*, we expand our vision beyond America's borders to bring together the voices of martial artists from across the globe. This book unites the experiences and philosophies of elite practitioners from the United States, Canada, the United Kingdom, and Australia, offering unique perspectives on how martial arts has shaped their lives and careers.

For the reader, this book is more than just a collection of stories—it is a blueprint for success, a source of inspiration, and a guide to personal transformation. Each chapter unveils invaluable life, business, and leadership lessons, providing wisdom that transcends cultures and backgrounds. Whether you are a martial artist, an entrepreneur, a leader, or someone seeking motivation, the principles within these pages are universally applicable.

Through these shared experiences, you will discover the secrets to success—how to cultivate resilience in the face of adversity, lead with integrity, and turn passion into purpose. Every story holds a lesson, and every insight has the potential to open new doors of opportunity and understanding.

As you embark on this journey through the minds and lives of some of the world's most dedicated martial artists, we invite you to absorb their wisdom, reflect on their experiences, and apply their teachings to your path. This book is not just about martial arts; it is about the art of living—a philosophy anyone can embrace, regardless of background or discipline.

Welcome to *Elite Martial Artists Worldwide: Secrets to Life, Leadership, and Business, Volume III*, where every page is a lesson, and every lesson is an opportunity for growth.

Let the journey begin...

SECRETS TO

LIFE

CHAPTER ONE

HOW MARTIAL ARTS PRINCIPLES CAN ENHANCE LEADERSHIP, BUSINESS & PERSONAL LIFE

BY JOHN CONNELLY

Training in martial arts is far more than just learning physical techniques—it is a discipline that cultivates valuable life skills, shaping the body, mind, and spirit. Through consistent practice, martial artists develop qualities that extend well beyond combat, influencing success in leadership, business, and personal growth.

From my own experience, I have found that regular training fosters several key attributes that contribute to both personal and professional success:

- **Discipline** – Martial arts instill a strong sense of discipline through consistent practice and adherence to principles. This translates into better self-control, time management, and perseverance in both professional and personal endeavors.

- **Focus** – The intense concentration required in training sharpens mental clarity, enhancing decision-making and productivity in daily life.
- **Resilience** – Overcoming physical and mental challenges in martial arts builds resilience and fortitude, preparing individuals to handle setbacks and difficulties with confidence.
- **Confidence** – Mastering techniques and progressing in skill level boosts self-confidence, which enhances performance in all areas of life.
- **Respect** – Martial arts fosters respect for instructors, peers, and the community, strengthening interpersonal relationships and promoting positive social interactions.
- **Goal-Setting** – Advancement in martial arts is structured around rank progression and skill development, reinforcing the importance of setting and achieving both short and long-term goals.
- **Self-Defense** – The ability to protect oneself provides peace of mind, reducing stress and increasing overall well-being.
- **Mental Calmness** – Breathing techniques and meditation, fundamental aspects of martial arts, promote emotional regulation, mindfulness, and inner peace.

In the following sections, I will explore each of these principles in greater depth, illustrating how martial arts benefits can be applied to business and leadership, as well as personal development.

① Discipline & Consistency

- **Martial Arts:** Discipline is a cornerstone of martial arts training. It often involves rigorous, repetitive practice. Mastery of a new move doesn't happen instantly—it requires consistent effort over time. In Taekwondo, for instance, practitioners must repeatedly practice kicks, strikes, and combinations until they become second nature. Continued practice ensures these skills are maintained at a high level. Through this consistent effort to perfect each technique, discipline is built, and with discipline, we can achieve successful outcomes.

- **In Business:** The principle of consistency in martial arts mirrors success in business. Howard Schultz, the former CEO of Starbucks, didn't build a global empire overnight. He consistently improved the product, ensured a consistent customer experience in every store, and maintained rigorous quality control. Success came from continuously refining processes and showing up day after day, even when the company was still a work in progress.

② Goal Setting

- **Martial Arts:** Every martial artist follows a personal roadmap, whether it's written down or committed to memory. These goals are always at the forefront of their minds, and they focus on the outcomes they wish to achieve. Taekwondo, Karate, and Judo, for example, start with the white belt and progress toward black belt status, with even further milestones at higher Dan levels. This journey isn't just about mastering techniques—it's about toughening the spirit and strengthening the body as practitioners advance in the art. Achieving this progress requires setting incremental goals and milestones.

  Some practitioners may choose to compete in tournaments for personal growth, while others focus on the mindfulness aspects of the practice. Regardless of the approach, these goals are often broken down into specific, measurable milestones, such as improving flexibility, increasing sparring skills, or enhancing overall fitness.

- **In Business:** The entrepreneurial journey of Sara Blakely, the founder of Spanx, exemplifies the power of goal-setting. Blakely's vision for a successful product was broken down into concrete steps. She meticulously perfected her product, tested it extensively, pitched it relentlessly to retailers, and built her brand from the ground up. Each goal she set helped her overcome challenges, eventually leading her to create a billion-dollar company.

③ **Resilience & Perseverance**

- **Martial Arts:** A key challenge in martial arts is learning to overcome failure and setbacks. For example, a Taekwondo competitor who loses multiple matches due to poor timing or decision-making may feel mentally discouraged. However, martial arts teach that setbacks are valuable learning experiences. A resilient competitor learns from their mistakes, analyses what went wrong, and returns to training stronger than before.

- **In Business:** The story of Steve Jobs and Apple is a powerful example of resilience. Jobs was famously fired from the company he founded, yet his perseverance led him to establish NeXT and Pixar. When Apple brought him back, he transformed the company into one of the world's most valuable enterprises. His ability to embrace personal setbacks and turn them into motivating forces was instrumental in his eventual success.

④ **Focus & Mental Toughness**

- **Martial Arts:** Focus is a foundational skill in martial arts. During sparring sessions, practitioners must adhere to their strategies while adeptly responding to their opponent's movements. In Karate Kumite (sparring), for instance, a lapse in focus can result in being struck. Developing the mental toughness to remain calm under pressure and execute techniques with precision is a gradual process honed over time.

- **In Business:** The capacity to maintain focus under pressure is equally vital in the business realm. Indra Nooyi, the former CEO of PepsiCo, exemplified this trait by making significant decisions in high-pressure environments. Her ability to eliminate distractions and concentrate on strategic objectives, such as diversifying PepsiCo's portfolio and promoting healthier products, was crucial to the company's direction. This mirrors the mental discipline martial artists employ during combat to stay on course.

⑤ **Adaptability & Problem-Solving**

- **Martial Arts:** Adaptability is essential in martial arts, particularly when confronting diverse opponents. For example, a wrestler may need to modify techniques when facing a taller adversary, or a boxer might adjust footwork against a more aggressive challenger. Being resourceful with available techniques and thinking swiftly are critical components of martial arts training.

- **In Business:** Adaptability is equally crucial in business. Netflix's evolution exemplifies this principle. Initially a DVD rental service, Netflix pivoted its business model as streaming technology became more viable. Recognising changes in the marketplace, the company embraced internet streaming and invested in original content, transforming it into a leading streaming platform. This strategic shift underscores the importance of recognising market dynamics and adapting accordingly, akin to a martial artist adjusting tactics based on the opponent.

⑥ **Leadership & Teamwork**

- **Martial Arts:** Leadership and teamwork are integral to many martial arts disciplines, especially those practised in schools or dojos. Higher-ranked students are often responsible for instructing lower-ranked peers, guiding them with patience, and demonstrating techniques. This mentorship fosters a culture of collaboration. Leadership is frequently assessed by one's ability to help others develop rather than solely by personal prowess.

- **In Business:** Companies like Google embody this collaborative leadership approach. Leaders are expected to cultivate environments that encourage idea-sharing and cross-departmental cooperation. Leadership involves empowering others, much like a martial arts sensei who inspires students to progress and innovate. When teams collaborate and respect each other's strengths, they achieve greater success collectively.

⑦ **Confidence & Self-Awareness**

- **Martial Arts:** Martial arts training fosters confidence by confronting fears and overcoming challenges. For instance, a jiu-jitsu practitioner may initially feel anxious about sparring with more experienced partners; however, through consistent training, they build confidence in their abilities. Additionally, martial arts cultivate self-awareness by helping individuals recognise their unique strengths and weaknesses, enabling them to manage their options effectively.

- **In Business:** Oprah Winfrey exemplifies the power of self-awareness in business. She transitioned from a talk show host to building a multimedia empire by recognising the value of her authenticity and her ability to connect deeply with audiences. This self-awareness allowed her to leverage her strengths effectively. In business, understanding one's capabilities is crucial for capitalising on strengths and seeking assistance in areas of weakness.

⑧ Stress Management

- **Martial Arts:** Martial arts disciplines often incorporate techniques such as controlled breathing and meditation to help practitioners maintain composure under pressure. Traditional forms like Tai Chi and Kung Fu emphasise slow, deliberate movements designed to calm the mind and centre the body, aiding in stress and anxiety management.

- **In Business:** High-stress leaders, such as Sheryl Sandberg, have openly discussed the importance of stress management. Sandberg emphasises mindfulness and taking moments to reset, especially in fast-paced business environments. Effective stress management enables leaders to maintain clarity, enhance decision-making, and preserve overall health. During critical business situations, calm and composed leaders often achieve superior results.

⑨ Time Management

- **Martial Arts:** Training in martial arts is time-intensive, teaching practitioners to maximise their efforts by balancing training with other commitments such as work, education, or family. This necessitates effective prioritisation and organisation. Successful martial artists schedule regular practice sessions and allocate time for technique refinement to ensure continuous progress.

- **In Business:** Elon Musk is renowned for his rigorous time management skills. He reportedly segments his day into five-minute intervals to maintain high productivity. Whether managing multiple enterprises or adhering to tight deadlines, Musk's meticulous scheduling ensures each task receives appropriate attention. The discipline required for effective time management is a trait shared by both successful business leaders and martial artists.

⑩ Respect & Integrity

- **Martial Arts:** Respect forms the cornerstone of martial arts. Practitioners demonstrate this through rituals such as bowing upon entering the dojo, showing deference to instructors and peers, and adhering to a strict code of conduct that instils humility. Integrity is equally vital, as students are taught to apply their skills responsibly and ethically.

- **In Business:** The company Patagonia exemplifies how integrity and respect for core values can lead to business success. Operating with a clear mission of environmental sustainability, founder Yvon Chouinard made bold decisions, such as donating a percentage of profits to environmental causes. Even when it meant sacrificing short-term gains, this commitment to ethical practices cultivated a loyal customer base. In business, acting with integrity fosters long-term trust and loyalty.

⑪ Calmness and Personal Ease through Breathing Techniques and Meditation

Incorporating breathing techniques and meditation into daily routines offers numerous benefits in both martial arts and business contexts.

- **Martial Arts:**
    - o Enhanced Focus and Mental Clarity: Meditation aids in eliminating distractions, sharpening mental focus, and improving attention to detail, which is crucial in martial arts where split-second decisions can determine outcomes.
    - o Stress Reduction and Emotional Control: Deep breathing techniques activate the parasympathetic nervous system, promoting relaxation and enabling practitioners to maintain composure under pressure. This control over stress and anxiety is vital during intense situations.
    - o Improved Physical Performance: Proper breathing enhances endurance and energy flow, facilitating better recovery during training. Efficient oxygen delivery to muscles allows martial artists to perform optimally, especially during demanding sessions.
    - o Optimised Energy Flow (Qi or Chi): Disciplines such as Tai Chi and Qigong emphasise the control and circulation of energy (Qi or Chi). Mastery of breath control directly influences this energy, contributing to a more effective practice.
    - o Strengthened Mind-Body Connection: Breathing techniques and meditation foster a

deeper connection between mind and body, enabling practitioners to better sense their movements and anticipate opponents' intentions, thereby enhancing reaction time and adaptability.

- **Business:**
  - o Improved Decision-Making and Problem-Solving: Meditation enhances cognitive functions, aiding individuals in making rational, clear-minded decisions. Maintaining calmness in the fast-paced business world is essential when facing high-stakes situations.
  - o Effective Stress Management: Business leaders often encounter high-stress levels. Regular practice of breathing techniques can help regulate stress, reducing the risk of burnout. A calm and collected leader inspires confidence and makes better decisions under pressure.
  - o Enhanced Focus and Productivity: Meditation improves concentration and the ability to stay on task. In business, focusing on important tasks while minimising distractions is key to productivity. Regular meditation sessions support sustained attention, even during extended working hours.
  - o Emotional Regulation and Resilience: Mindfulness practices increase awareness of one's emotions and reactions. In a business context, this translates to better emotional regulation, facilitating effective leadership, conflict resolution, and the cultivation of strong relationships with clients and colleagues.
  - o Fostering Creativity and Innovation: Meditation encourages openness and receptivity. By calming the mind, it allows for

greater creativity, enabling individuals to generate innovative ideas and approach challenges from fresh perspectives.

o Enhanced Health and Energy Levels: Consistent practice of breathing exercises and meditation can improve overall physical and mental health. Benefits include increased energy levels, better sleep quality, and reduced illness-related absences, all of which are crucial for maintaining long-term productivity and business success.

Integrating these practices into daily routines can lead to significant improvements in both personal well-being and professional performance.

Conclusion:

Martial arts transcend physical prowess, imparting valuable life, leadership, and business skills. The core principles of discipline, focus, resilience, leadership, adaptability, and respect cultivate personal and professional growth. Embracing martial arts philosophy and practices enables individuals to evolve into better versions of themselves, applying these lessons to everyday life, business, and personal development, thereby achieving growth, accomplishment, and lasting success.

May your martial arts journey unveil the secrets to success in all facets of life.

ABOUT JOHN CONNELLY

AUSTRALIA

Master John Connelly stands as a distinguished master instructor from Australia, renowned for his illustrious career in education spanning back to 1997. With over two decades of expertise in instructing, coaching, and teaching martial arts, he has gained recognition as a United States Open International Medalist. Currently, he serves as the Head Instructor at SMAC Tang Soo Do School in Mareeba, Queensland, and also holds the esteemed position of Head Instructor at Sports Martial Arts Combat (SMAC). Master Connelly exemplifies excellence in martial arts leadership, and his inclusion in Elite Martial Artists Worldwide Volume III highlights his exceptional skills and contributions to the field.

FOR MORE INFORMATION:

- SMAC Sports Martial Arts Combat
- Website: www.movingwell.org

CHAPTER TWO

THE RELATIONSHIPS THAT DEVELOPED A LEADER

BY RON DARGAN

Love. Love is a warm thing; love is an emotion. Without love, this world would be full of darkness and hate because love brightens up things.

Those were the opening lines to the poem I recited at my 3rd-grade graduation. A moment that would change the way I saw myself forever.

As a shy young man growing up in Philadelphia, I had mastered the art of blending into the background. I wasn't the kid who raised his hand in class. I wasn't the one who cracked jokes or demanded attention. I was the observer - the one who listened more than he spoke and let others take center stage while I stayed in the wings.

But three elementary school teachers saw something in me that I hadn't yet seen in myself. They believed I had a voice worth sharing and were determined to ensure I used it.

At first, I resisted. The thought of standing in front of the entire audience, speaking into a microphone, sent waves of anxiety through me. What if I stuttered? What if my voice cracked? What if I forgot the words? But my teachers didn't let me run from the opportunity. They encouraged, guided, and, most of all, made me believe my words mattered.

The day of graduation arrived. My heart pounded as I walked onto the stage. Rows of parents, teachers, and classmates sat before me, waiting. The spotlight was on me now, and there was no turning back. I took a deep breath and spoke.

"Love, Love is a warm thing...."

With each word, I felt the fear melting away. I focused on the message, on the power of love that brings light into darkness, to turn hate into hope. And when I finished, the silence was replaced with applause. At that moment, I understood what teachers had seen in me all along. I wasn't just a shy kid from Philadelphia. I had a voice. I had something to say, and when I spoke, people listened. The poem about love was more than words; it was the beginning of my journey toward confidence and embracing my place in the world. And it all started with three teachers who refused to let me stay invisible.

My Martial Arts Journey

In March 1970, my mother and I visited a relative who happens to be a third-degree blackbelt, my uncle Persival Outland. I was 10 and ready to start my karate journey. I would leave my friends on the basketball court, grab my Gi, and walk 5 miles for practice. See Kin Do Karate was the style, which I found out years later was a spin-off of the discipline he learned, Taekwondo.

This is the point at which a change took place in my childhood. The shy kid was now teaching karate to his siblings and neighborhood friends.

Four Reasons People Change:

① Hurt enough - they have to

② See enough - they're inspired to

③ Learn enough - they want to

④ Received enough - they're able to

I'm entering high school, and my karate training is on hold. My focus was baseball, football, and, on a lesser scale, girls.

The focus, discipline, and respect I learned from karate helped me earn two varsity letters, an MVP in football and baseball, and an Honorable Mention All-Public in baseball.

The Decision

Working a 9-5 or going to college didn't inspire me. On April 20 (my mother's birthday), I received a package from Uncle Sam. The last information I read about was the Marine Corps, and I knew right away this was the one for me.

So, I called, and they had me at hello! The most angelic voice I've ever heard. I don't know what Sgt. Brown said, but being a teenager, I heard, "We have a date." Wearing my brown shark skin pants, brown silk shirt, and a splash of Hi Karate cologne, I poked my head into the office; I very smoothly asked for Sgt Brown. And there it was again, that angelic voice. "I'm Sgt Brown." My eyes almost popped, and my mouth dropped. That angelic voice couldn't be coming out of that face. I wanted to moonwalk like Michael Jackson out of there, but I felt committed. I shipped off for boot camp on August 15, 1978.

One of my recruiters told me about a well-known instructor in Jacksonville, NC, named Richard Gonzalez. After boot camp, I went to Jacksonville and started training again. Ferguson the Snake, my warehouse Sergeant-In-Charge, became my karate instructor. Soon, he started training under Richard Gonzalez in April 1979. He invited me in, and I never left.

Sensei Gonzalez was everything I was looking for in an instructor. I was in awe learning the history of Okinawa Kenpo and all the previous black belts like Larry Isaac, Vic Coffin, George Epps, and Al Louis.

Passing The Torch

Sensei Gonzalez left for Hawaii and turned the school over to Harry Wilburn, who turned it over to Al Louis, who later handed the keys to me. My training partner and friend, Greg Hargrave, came aboard as co-owner and Chief Instructor.

My Friendship with Ron Dargan

I met Ron in 1977 while we served at New River Air Station in N.C. We lived next door, and our wives were best friends. I was his best man at his wedding, and he was mine. Ron refuses to lose, even though losing is part of winning. Ron always set super high standards, and that attitude rubbed off on me. We started as white belts and were awarded our black belts together. - Greg Hargraves

July 26, 1980 - I Do

It was one of the best decisions I've ever made. At 19, I married my childhood sweetheart, Carolyn Elise Harris.

Fatherhood

Ronnie "Champ" Dargan II

Take a minute to reminisce about your life growing up. Was it in a lower economic status and poverty-stricken area, where trashy streets and abandoned buildings are not even eye sores but normal living? Imagine your neighborhood playground, where kids are expected to have the time of their lives, is also a war zone and death trap. And your daily living experience is infested with alcohol and drugs, gangs, criminals, and violence.

It's exceptionally inspiring for someone to escape that reality unscathed. But how? Especially seeing it firsthand and being surrounded by it during the most impressionable and developmental stages of their life. Experiencing this type of lifestyle will literally make or break you! Aside from any celebrity or athlete, this was only to set the tone for what was to come in the lives of those I admired and respected the most.

My father (aka Pops) inspired my life. And that accounts for all aspects of my life - from the simple way he talks to and treats people to his relentless work ethic and dedication. I've always considered myself extremely blessed, having lived half my life under that same roof as my role model. And to this day, he's always been as easy as a text/phone call away.

All that was shared about my father will most likely go to his head and boost his ego, but the Dargan family knows that next to the man above, his success is due to one key person who's always been in his life. So, thank you to the beautiful Mrs. Carolyn Elise Dargan.

Cedric Marqueth Dargan (Superstar)

"Success is when preparation meets opportunity."-Ron Dargan, my father

My father is, by far, the most successful man I know. I've seen him outplay and outshine people in sports and activities they've been doing for five years, even if he has only been doing it for five months.

When we were young, he told my brother and me that the key to success is when preparation meets opportunity. That statement has always stuck with me because my father used to quiz me on it. We could be riding in the car, and my father would say, "What's the key to success?" and I would have to respond, "When preparation meets opportunity.". I'm grateful he did this because my belief in this statement has been the key to my success in school, sports, and occupations.

I was successful in high school and college not because I was extremely smart but because of my preparation. I tried to complete every class and homework assignment, and I took down every note because I knew these things would help me succeed when it was time to take any type of assessment.

I was the only player from my high school team to play Division I Football, not because I was the best athlete on the team. It was due to my preparation during the off-season. My father inspired the work and the time I spent.

Paying It Back

Ron Dargan has been a mentor, role model, and friend for over 40 years. I met Ron while we were serving as US Marines in Kaneohe, Hawaii. A friend invited me to a warehouse martial arts class one night, and I was hooked immediately. Ron trained me from white to black belt, and then he received orders to the drill field. He'd made such an amazing impact on my life that I continued training for the next 35 years.

After leaving the Marine Corps, I opened two schools and convinced Ron to retire from the Marines after 25 years of service to help me run them. We trained and studied both martial arts and business around the country. We created five schools with nearly 850 students at its peak, graduating over 1000 1st-6th degree black belts, with Ron serving as the Chief Instructor of our organization.

From the moment I met Ron to this day, I have always said that everything he touches turns to gold.

- Kyoshi Brian DeGori, successful businessman, mentor, and investor.

From a Lamb to a Lion

While reading an article in a Marine Corps magazine about my former instructor, Ferguson the Snake, who is now the Hand-to-Hand Combat Instructor at Parris Island, SC, the next goal I must pursue came to me. I soon approached my First Sergeant. He hit me with news that felt like a punch in the gut. I must become a drill instructor and then apply for a hand-to-hand combat instructor. Being a DI was not in the cards.

The DI

Imagine driving through the base and observing Marines talking and yelling at trees. That's part of the DI training.

My Recruits

I was a Marine recruit during Mr. Dargan's tenure as a Drill Instructor. He is a proven leader that builds the confidence of anyone in his presence. I learned that Drill Instructor Sgt

Dargan was determined to master his craft and would not accept anything less from his recruits. One of the greatest takeaways that I have had since meeting Mr. Dargan is the importance and power of presentation. I can plainly hear my Drill Instructors voice as he would state "You can either be smart and fast, or dumb and strong!".

-Tony Lancaster, United States Marine Corps Veteran

Man, Myth, Legend

Many people know Hanshi Ron Dargan as a distinguished martial artist and mentor who profoundly impacted the martial arts community. However, before dedicating himself entirely to martial arts, Hanshi Dargan served as a Marine Corps Drill Instructor, where he honed his leadership skills and instilled discipline and resilience in countless recruits by reminding them that "You owe me, Private. Come down to Sgt Dargan's discotech where you can flop and drop while I dig you till your heart stops!"

-Bob Godwin, USMC (Ret), Doctorate of Ministry, Doctorate of Philosophy, PhD

Epitome of Awesomeotomy

My brother and friend who inspired me. He was, in my opinion, the best Drill Instructor, Career Recruiter, and Sgt Maj I knew. His name is Sgt. Maj Fenton Devil Dog Reese.

Hand-to-Hand Combat

After serving as a drill instructor, I became the top hand-to-hand combat instructor on Parris Island. I taught all three combat programs when it was just shoulder and hip throws. Pugil stick and bayonet training, then transition to the line, and now MCMAP.

Family Values

Justin James, Holly James, Justin II, Jabriel

MSgt USMC (Retired)

Sgt Dargan always had collateral duties as a Marine such as Combat Instructor, Officer Candidate School Instructor for young 2nd Lieutenants. He started martial arts classes for new beginners such as myself. I obtained a yellow belt throughout my lifetime of training.

No doubt, if you are reading this book about Mr. Ron Dargan, you will be inspired to achieve more. God and family values are very important to him and his family, and we believe in them. Be encouraged in the Lord as we are by having good examples such as the Dargan Family.

ABOUT RON DARGAN

USA

Bio/CV:

- Hanshi Ron Dargan 9th Degree Black Belt
- 1970-1975: Student, See Kin Do American Karate
- 1978: Graduated Marine Corps Boot Camp with Honors
- 1980: Trained with 10th Degree Grand Master Odo
- 1983-1984: Hawaii State Top Black Belt in kata, Weapons, & Fighting
- 1986-1987: Marine Corps. Hand-to-Hand Combat Instructor, Parris Island SC; Okinawa, Japan; Quantico, VA
- 1997: Mr. Torii Station Body Building Champion, Okinawa, Japan
- 1998: Mr. Far East Overall Body Building Champion, Okinawa, Japan
- 1999-2004: Grand Champion, Valentine Day Classic; Halloween Classic, North Carolina Nationals
- 2000: Hall of Fame World Karate Union, Pocono, PA
- 2002: Black Belt Marine Corps. Martial Arts Program

- 2003: Retired Marine Corps. Veteran, 25 years Master Sergeant
- 2015: VITA Saana BITMA Award, Outstanding selfless contributions
- 2023: Atlantic City Pickleball Tournament, 1st Singles (Golden Ticket); 1st Men's Doubles (Golden Ticket) w/ Stu Potter
- 2023: Starred in a movie as Lobby Guard #1 (Call Her King)
- 2024: Starred in my second movie role as a prison guard (The Father of Fentanyl)

FOR MORE INFORMATION:

- Okinawa Kenpo Karate Academy
- Website: www.okkawestdeptford.com
- Email: hanshi9@comcast.net
- Facebook: @okkawestdeptford

CHAPTER THREE

THE MAGIC INGREDIENT TO HAVING A SUCCESSFUL LIFE

BY JUANITA KAPP

I have walked the earth for 44 years and have learned many valuable life lessons. It is my wish to bring upliftment to the world, so I will share my life secrets with you in this chapter.

I believe we are called to live a certain life here on earth. We all have a special purpose, and there is a specific place for us in this timeline and reality that no one else can fulfill. That strengthens my belief that we were all born with a specific destiny put into place by our Creator, God Almighty, even before He laid the foundations of the earth.

Ephesians 1:4 New King James Version

4 Just as He chose us in Him before the foundation of the world, that we should be holy and without blame before Him in love.

The trials and tribulations that we go through in our journey shape and mold us into who we are to become. We are faced with many obstacles, trials, and tribulations, but we can never forget about the incredible miracles, blessings, and breakthroughs that transpire from these tests that we endure. You see, it's not just about reaching the summit of that mountain of personal victory; it is also about how we conduct ourselves whilst we are still in the valley. It's about how we treat others and especially how we treat ourselves.

What type of self-talk do we practise when faced with detrimental choices that we have to make for the good of our family, business, and life? What kind of self-love do we practise when we sometimes have to walk alone? How do we stay focused, and how do we encourage ourselves to surmount problematic situations in an eloquent way?

To me, the key to being a good person is to be kind to ourselves and others. I firmly believe in the scripture that says that if we can't say something positive, we should rather hold our tongue and keep our thoughts to ourselves.

Ephesians 4:29 New King James Version

[29] *Let no corrupt word proceed out of your mouth, but what is good for necessary edification, that it may impart grace to the hearers.*

Our thoughts, our words, and our actions all generate energy and facilitate the trajectory of our day. Where focus goes, energy flows so it is a part of my daily mantra to put good energy out there in the world through everything I do in my daily routine. It is important that we are cognisant of the frequency at which we operate.

I believe that emotion is energy in motion. The energy we create with our emotions can transcend even the most difficult tasks. We can literally break the negative mountains of life by exerting positive energy. We can do whatever we aim to do just by being positive. I believe in the power of the Word of God.

I also believe in science because it is a gift from God. I have done extensive research about the power of our words. I did not limit my research to only a religious perspective but also from a scientific point of view. As an ordained pastor for 15 years within the Full Gospel Church of God and a martial artist for almost a decade, I had the privilege of learning and understanding energy from different perspectives.

As a believer, I believe in the indwelling of the Holy Spirit of God. I believe that the Holy Spirit generates power and energy within us through the Trinity of the Bible: God the Father, God the Son, and God the Holy Spirit. I base this belief on the following scripture:

Romans 8:11New King James Version

[11] *But if the Spirit of Him who raised Jesus from the dead dwells in you, He who raised Christ from the dead will also give life to your mortal bodies through His Spirit who dwells in you.*

I found this experience not only in the church where I ministered and served full time for 15 years, I found it in my journey as a martial artist. I felt and saw the power of God at work through prayer and the preaching of scripture, especially in worship. I felt that same kind of power whilst doing martial arts. I felt and experienced the inner power that is generated from deep within my being while practising martial arts. I can't put it into words. It is powerful, it is intense, it is life-changing. It shook me to the core in wonderful ways. It aligned my body, soul, and spirit. It showed me what I am capable of and who I want to be in this world.

In religious terms, the power and energy that I described are generated by the Holy Spirit. In martial arts terms, I believe that the power within I am describing is what we call "ki" or "chi". To me, it is the same thing. I have fought many martial artists, and when I do, I feel their "ki" resonating; it's almost as if I can see it with my own eyes. I base my belief and conviction on this via the following scripture:

Romans 8:16 New King James Version

16 *The Spirit Himself bears witness with our spirit that we are children of God,*

Why do I say this? Something happens to me when I meet a fellow believer and a fellow martial artist. It doesn't matter what the situation or the occasion is; without saying a single word or having a conversation, I can tell you which individuals in the room are believers and/or martial artists. I say this confidently because I don't need my eyes to see it or words to hear it; I simply feel it. That is the power of the Holy Spirit, that is the power of "ki."

Hence, it is my pleasure to share my secrets about life in this chapter, as I know that the audience is comprised of martial artists who are also believers. If you are reading this and you don't fall into either of these categories, I would encourage you to "eat the fish and spit out the bones."

What is my definition of living a successful life? It is the following:

- To "tame the pen and the sword"
- To find your passion in life and fulfill your destiny
- To find happiness

To me, possessions and everything that goes with a high-profile lifestyle don't matter much. What matters to me is the people I meet and how I can positively impact them. When I work with people, I am happy. That, to me, is the true essence of being successful. I feel successful when I positively create impact and influence.

My magic ingredients for a successful life are below:

① **Be kind.**

Being kind to others is a powerful tool to shape your character. Don't just be kind to other kind people, be kind to the nasty people out there that want to destroy you and that talk behind your back. They are behind you for a reason. Your kindness might just teach them to become a better person. Never hold a grudge; instead, choose peace, love, and kindness.

② **Let the sunshine glow over others.**

Never try to short-circuit the success of others. There is enough space and opportunities for us all. Let the sunshine glow over others as much as possible. Other people need good breaks in life just like you do. The more you help others; the more doors will open for you. On top of that, God will bless you because you give freely and without expecting something back. This is the type of spiritual return on investment that God talks about in His word:

Luke 6:38 New King James Version

[38] *Give, and it will be given to you: good measure, pressed down, shaken together, and running over will be put into your bosom. For with the same measure that you use, it will be measured back to you.*

③ **Be positive.**

Negativity chases people away. Instead of spending so much time being negative, you can flip the script and be positive instead. There is always a harvest on what you sow. If you sow negativity, that energy will be returned to you. If you sow positive vibes, that is what you will receive in return. Being positive doesn't cost you anything but the result of it will bless you in tremendous ways because that positive energy will accumulate and multiply exponentially.

④ **Learn from your mistakes.**

If you made a mistake, it only means you were given an opportunity to learn a new lesson. That is exactly what you should do, you should learn from it. Don't let your mistakes define you; let your learning experiences help you to create your legacy. You can choose what people will remember about you.

⑤ **Treat others with dignity.**

I treat all individuals the same way, whether they are high-level professionals or celebrities or they clean the airports that I frequent during my travels. You get the idea.

⑥ **Don't compete with others; compete with yourself.**

People start competing with others when they compare themselves to them. Don't compare yourself to others. It will only result in petty arguments or thoughts and will end up being a thorn in your side. Compete only with yourself. Everyone is on their own journey. Remember to cheer others on. They deserve it. They are also working hard behind the scenes to fulfill their dreams.

⑦ **Be consistent.**

Do what you say and say what you do, and repeat that for the rest of your life. Be consistent in who you are and what you stand for.

⑧ **Live with integrity.**

Be the same person you are when you are singing praises in church than when you are shopping or spending time with your family behind closed doors. Live with integrity; it will lengthen your years here on earth. Being fake takes too much effort and does nothing positive for your character.

⑨ **Stick to your morals and values.**

Don't be pressured into following new trends that can harm your body, mind, or peace. Protect your peace by sticking to your morals and values.

⑩ **Be a good person.**

You know the difference between what is right and what is wrong. Choose to do the right thing in every decision you make.

⑪ **Love yourself.**

Don't be self-absorbed; instead, be good to yourself and love yourself. Look after your physical health as well as your mental health.

⑫ **Love others.**

Do right by others. Treat them like you want them to treat you. Respect their boundaries and help them where you can. This is God's will for you.

⑬ **Love life.**

Be grateful for the chance you have every day to live. It is a gift from God. Treat it like one. Unwrap it every morning and enjoy it to the fullest.

⑭ Be yourself.

Just be—no pretending and nonsense. Just be yourself and be happy about it.

⑮ Give honour where honour is due.

Never forget to celebrate the accomplishments of others. Not everything is about you all the time.

⑯ Smile.

Smiling is like medicine to your soul. Your smile can change someone else's day for the better.

⑰ Work hard.

Nothing beats the feeling of reaching an accomplishment when you know that you worked hard for it. Work hard every single day, and you will see the fruit of your labour.

⑱ Bless others.

If you have the resources and the opportunity to help someone along their path, do it without thinking twice. There is not only a physical reward in doing this, but also a personal development that takes place which is priceless.

⑲ Respect is everything.

If you don't have respect for yourself, then you will not have respect for others. Learn to respect yourself before you attempt to respect others. Everything in life is about respect. When I think of the essence of respect, I think of the following scripture:

John 14:6 New King James Version

[6] *Jesus said to him, "I am the way, the truth, and the life. No one comes to the Father except through Me."*

John Maxwell wrote this when John 14:6 inspired him; he said: "Know the way, show the way, and go the way."

If you want to work on the essence of showing respect to others in your life, then "Know the way" of respect – learn what it entails. "Go the way" of respect – practise what you have learned and "show the way" – teach others you meet about your personal journey about respect.

Above all, remember that the magic ingredient to having a successful life is to LIVE IT. So go out and live, don't just exist.

Should you wish to collaborate with me on any projects, kindly visit my website, www.meticulousmoments.com, and fill in the contact form.

God bless you all.

Osu!

ABOUT JUANITA KAPP

SOUTH AFRICA

Bio/CV:

- Founder & Owner of the Meticulous Moments Show, Meticulous Martial Arts Mastermind (MMAM) & the MMAM Hall of Fame
- Co-Host Joe Cortez Show: The Happy Hour
- Co-Founder KAPPTOR Connection, Business Prowess Podcast
- 7 X International Best-Selling Author
- Author of "Lioness: A Warrior's Journey"
- Hoinser Media Group Brand Ambassador & Media Correspondent (Europe)
- Hoinser Media Group Award - Exceptional Leader of Excellence 2023
- Global Public Speaker & MC
- Spiritual Counselor (Level 5 Religious Professional)
- Ordained Pastor
- Martial Artist (3rd Dan Tang Soo Do) & Brown Belt 2 in Shorin-Ryu Shorinkan
- UK Black Belt Hall of Famer
- Spartan Hall of Warriors President SA

Inducted into:

- Action Martial Arts Hall of Fame
- The UK Martial Arts Hall of Fame
- International Martial Arts Hall of Fame
- UMAHOF Hall of Fame Inductee
- MMAM Hall of Fame Inductee 2024
- Williams Hall of Honors
- Williams Hall of Honors

Other accolades:

- TYGA Martial Arts International Member (UK)
- Media Correspondent Rage Global Entertainment
- Boss "No Confusion Records" – UK
- History General Sports Karate Museum Archives
- Global Ambassador World Bushido Foundation
- Media Correspondent Come On In Elite Global Foundation
- Received the American Flag from the Come On In Elite Global Foundation
- Awarded medal by the WBC
- Executive Producer & Stunt Coordinator
- Film Agent
- Actress

FOR MORE INFORMATION:

- Email: meticulousmacarons@gmail.com
- Website: www.meticulousmoments.com
- Facebook: @juanita.kapp.54
- Instagram: @juanita_kapp
- LinkedIn: @juanita-kapp-904243199
- TikTok: @meticulous.macarons2020

CHAPTER FOUR

INTENT INTO ACTION PART II

BY TODD NORCROSS

"This is a follow-up to the chapter "Intent into Action" in the book Elite Martial Artists in America Volume II

Preface: As a martial artist, I aim to improve a little each day, striving to be better than I was yesterday. When I write or offer advice, I am primarily speaking to myself. I acknowledge that I have many failures and faults. Though I often fall short, I focus on mastering eight key principles. Throughout my forty-five years of practicing Budo, I have learned a crucial life lesson: never stop learning; always remain a student.

① Practice Gratitude Every Day

Reflecting on gratitude helps put things into perspective. It brings us peace of mind and makes it easier to feel content. It encourages positive thinking and enhances our mental well-being. Additionally, it calms our emotions and improves our daily relationships.

Gratitude is a two-way street. The person who gives should not remember. The person who receives should never forget it.

Reflecting daily on gratitude can change our perspective from what we lack to the abundance in our lives. We rarely complain when we consider how some individuals live in extreme poverty, whether across the globe or right in our own neighborhoods. It's important to recognize that somewhere, someone would give everything they have for the things we often take for granted.

Action:

Write down your blessings. It is a wonderful habit to take time each day to write down or reflect on at least three things we are grateful for. This practice can help cultivate a mindset of appreciation. Instead of (or in addition to) a New Year's resolution, consider creating a detailed list of everything you already have. Keep that list throughout the new year and display it in a place where you can see it often. Whenever you feel down or discouraged, refer to this gratitude list. It serves as a reminder to awaken us to contentment and appreciation for life, with all its abundance and opportunities.

② Set Goals to Discover a Purpose

How often do we come home from work or school and choose to just lay around and do nothing? We all have days like this. While a restful day can be refreshing occasionally, we know that these "lazy days" are not the best use of our limited time on Earth. It's perfectly fine to set aside one or two days a month for naps and binge-watching our favorite shows, but for the rest of the time, we should engage in activities that challenge and fulfill us. Research shows that having a sense of purpose and working toward something meaningful brings both the heart and mind great satisfaction.

A Challenge:

We can acknowledge and appreciate even the smallest personal victories. By stacking up these little successes, we can create a tsunami-like momentum of unstoppable achievement. It's important to focus on our progress, no matter how minor, as this mindset helps us feel positive and motivated. If we only dwell on our potential and complain to friends about our troubles and failures, we'll miss the opportunity to see the light and escape the nihilistic trap of everyday life. Time passes quickly, so let's set new goals and work to achieve them today.

③ Stay Here and Now

The future hasn't occurred yet, so why do we make assumptions about it? Our minds can often waste time thinking instead of acting. We tend to envision our future because we may not be content with our present. Fantasizing about what could be often feels more appealing than facing reality. If we constantly yearn for what tomorrow might bring, we risk overlooking the beauty of today. We need to appreciate the wonderful moments that surround us right now.

A Daily Meditation:

Sit down and smile. Focus on being present in the moment. Engaging in daily mindfulness practices, such as Zen meditation or simply taking a moment to slow down and express gratitude, can enhance our appreciation for everyday experiences.

We can spend just ten minutes concentrating on our breathing. When distracting thoughts arise, acknowledge them and then gently let them go, returning your focus to your breath. Repeat this process continuously and pay attention to how you feel. Notice your blood pressure and heart rate begin to decrease. Observe the stillness that emerges and recognize how this practice puts you in control.

It's remarkable how much this daily habit can help relax the body and alleviate accumulated stress. Try it for a week or two and see how you feel. Over time, this practice can help reduce anxious thoughts about the past or future. This doesn't mean we shouldn't prepare for what lies ahead; it simply means we should not overlook the gift of today.

④ Take Care of Your Physical Health

I would be a hypocrite if I did not include this, as it directly relates to overall well-being. Every health expert emphasizes the importance of regularly exercising, eating well, and ensuring adequate hydration and rest. We all know this is true, yet we often struggle to adhere to these guidelines.

Personally, I tend to overeat. I was raised on inexpensive, processed foods, and I typically get only about five hours of sleep each night. My workdays often stretch to fourteen hours. I probably don't drink nearly enough water, either.

While I am aware of these issues, I strive to discipline myself to maintain a healthy body weight. I make an effort to keep moving and stretching, especially since I am in my mid-fifties. However, I often fall short of my goals. So, who am I to offer advice on this? Well, I'm not claiming to be an expert. However, the advice to prioritize health and well-being has always been sound and true. It can be found in every self-help book and health brochure available, so I feel it's important to include it in this book as well.

Keep Moving:

We can truly feel the effects of exercise. It releases endorphins that help combat stress. Our physical health directly impacts our emotional well-being, allowing us to maintain balance in our moods. This is a constant struggle for many of us, but the good news is that we can choose to change our habits at any time. Movement is free.

⑤ Stop Comparing Yourself to Others

At times, we can look at the lives of others as an inspiring way to modify our own. Healthy competition can ignite creativity and innovation, which ultimately enhance society and improve humanity. This is the positive aspect of comparison.

Long ago, when humanity was still young, competition likely played a crucial role in helping us become valued and accepted members of our clans. If we were seen as "useless" by those in power, we risked being cast out of our caves or societies—away from the warmth of the fire—and left to fend for ourselves, potentially facing death in the cold.

Fortunately, in the 21st century, most of us live in relatively safe and abundant times. However, this extreme comfort can lead to idleness and boredom. Many people turn to the internet to find their identity, particularly on social media. If we feel lonely or overlooked, we might be tempted to post heavily filtered selfies to gain as many "likes" as possible. While this behavior may seem ridiculous and narcissistic, it is something many engage in. These fleeting moments of approval provide a temporary boost of dopamine, leading us to repeat the behavior over and over. Eventually, our desire for validation can transform into an unhealthy addiction.

If you like yourself, why seek others' approval? Be yourself intentionally.

Excessive comparison to others can lead to destructive feelings of inadequacy, disconnection, and jealousy. Over time, we may start to feel that our lives are not good enough. Some individuals may even prioritize their desires over grace and morality. This puts us at risk of becoming victims of the modern "look at me" culture, causing us to perceive everyone around us as less than perfect and to covet what belongs to others.

Instead of feeling envious of those we follow on social media, we can choose to log off our devices and focus on our own journey and family. It's easy to judge others' faults while overlooking our own. A busy person hardly has time to feel jealous, and a truly happy person has no time for it at all.

Unplug and disconnect as much as possible and return to a simple life on Earth. Turn off machines before they turn against you.

⑥ **Give to Others:**

"To ease another's heartache is to forget one's own." – Abraham Lincoln

Action:

Give It Away. Performing genuine acts of kindness and volunteering has been shown to increase feelings of fulfillment and happiness. Helping each other fosters a sense of community and belonging. We can volunteer one afternoon each month at a local food pantry. We can take our kids to rake leaves for an elderly neighbor. If we can afford it, we can donate money or gifts to causes and charities that we believe in. Afterward, we should avoid feeding our egos by seeking public recognition for our deeds; the acts themselves are the true reward. If we engage in random acts of kindness, we are likely to feel less lonely and disconnected. While it is easy to accumulate more property or give money to impress others, it is far better to create a space in our hearts— however small—where we act out of love and generosity rather than envy or greed.

⑦ Live with Realistic Expectations

Many relationships involve one person holding unrealistic expectations. Lacking self-esteem, they attempt to mold and control the thoughts and lifestyles of others to match their desires. This can manifest through mind games, intimidation, manipulation, and sometimes even outright abuse as they try to change the other person into someone they are not. This behavior exemplifies living with excessively unrealistic expectations.

Perfection doesn't exist:

When we demand perfection, we create unnecessary stress and anxiety where it isn't needed. Life is beautifully imperfect, and we should accept that. It's a journey filled with ups and downs, unexpected losses, suffering, regret, love, beauty, and triumph—all of which are integral parts of our experience. This is simply how life is meant to be. As one of my teachers once said, "An enlightened perspective comes when we lower our expectations to align with reality." I believe that the more we cling to the idea that perfection will bring us happiness, the more disappointed we will be. We'll end up feeling argumentative and frustrated all the time, which can push others away—leading us to be all thorns and no roses.

Embrace every bump and scratch that life throws at us. The moment we stop expecting perfection from circumstances, other people, or ourselves, we will discover all of the hidden beauty within the chaos.

⑧ Stay Positive

Have you ever felt the urge to punch someone in the face? You know, the person who is always grinning, annoyingly perky, and seemingly fake in their happiness? It's a common feeling. But what is their secret? Are they blissfully unaware of how difficult life can be, or do some people simply choose to stay "on the bright side" regardless of the challenges they face? Perhaps they are onto something. They may have discovered the key to viewing adversity not as an obstacle, but as an opportunity for growth and learning.

I believe that this optimistic mindset is something we can all strive to adopt. It reflects a sense of faith and courage, teaching us to focus on hope like a candle flickering in the dark.

Maintaining an optimistic attitude helps us frame our challenges positively and empowers us to keep moving forward, even when sadness feels overwhelming. The world could always use more joy, brightness, and hope.

It is my sincerest wish that all who read this book discover inner peace, outward love, and enigmatic answers.

ABOUT TODD NORCROSS

USA

Bio/CV:

- Bujinkan Budo (9th dan) - Sakki Test given by Dai Shihan Arnaud Cousergue (France)
- Budo Taijutsu Shihan 9th dan (Hanshi)
- Karate Shodan in 1987
- Record Engineering Degree 1997
- Awarded Bujinkan Shidoshi teaching license by Soke Masaaki Hatsumi in Japan
- Presented the Eastern Name 'Ho-Un' (Dharma Cloud) in 2004
- To-Shin Do (3rd Dan in 2007) awarded by Stephen K. Hayes
- Bachelor's Degree in Philosophy
- Awarded the Toshi Order Warrior Name 'Ryotoshi' (Knight of the Bright Blade of Truth) in 2007
- Member of the Marishi-Kai Protectors Guild
- Bodyguard for the Dalai Lama, Muhammad Ali, and other celebrities and dignitaries.

- Has taught self-defense courses for local and state law enforcement, the U.S. Military, and various public and private school systems.
- Author of "The Dojo Martial Arts Curriculum" and more than a dozen weapons courses.
- Musician/Producer of over 32 albums of original music.
- Since 2006, owns and teaches at The Dojo - A Black Belt Budo School in Mason, Ohio.

FOR SEMINARS & SPEAKING ENGAGEMENTS:

- Email: thedojocincinnati@gmail.com
- YouTube Channel (35k subscribers): YouTube/The Dojo Martial Arts
- Full Music Catalog: Todd Norcross on Spotify or Amazon Music

CHAPTER FIVE

KEEPING A GROWTH MINDSET: THE KEY TO LIFELONG SUCCESS

BY JESSICA C. PHILLIPS

Introduction

I didn't give much thought to the term *growth mindset* until adulthood. It wasn't until I enrolled in college as an adult learner that I encountered it—and soon, it influenced my decision-making, thinking, and overall approach to life. The more I reflected on it, the more it wove into my daily habits, particularly my martial arts journey.

When I began martial arts as a white belt in 2019, I had no idea how many times I would need to reset my thinking, challenge my limits, and make the conscious decision to *show up*. Earning my first-degree black belt was not just about physical endurance; it was a mental battle. The night before my test, doubt crept in. My thoughts scattered, and I questioned whether I had what it took to pass. What if I failed? How could I silence the fear?

A Growth Mindset.

That, combined with prayer, redirected my thoughts and kept me from spiraling into negativity. One of my favorite scriptures came to mind: *"I can do all things through Christ who strengthens me"* (Philippians 4:13). With a clear mind and renewed determination, I passed my black belt test. That moment remains etched in my heart—not just for the achievement but for the perseverance it took to get there. It taught me a valuable lesson—success isn't just about skill or strength; it's about mindset. Time and time again, I've realized that the biggest obstacles aren't external but internal, rooted in the doubts and fears we allow to take hold.

Overcoming mental roadblocks—imposter syndrome, self-doubt, past emotional wounds, fear of the unknown, anxiety, or comparison—demands a growth mindset. It takes one decision to push forward, to believe in yourself, and to take that next step. That one choice can be the difference between stagnation and progress—between giving up and stepping into the greatness you were meant for.

I'm reminded of an image I once saw online. It depicted a man mining, just inches away from striking a diamond. Yet, at the brink of success, he gave up and walked away, never realizing how close he was. That image has stayed with me as a reminder: you will never reach your full potential if you quit, run from challenges, or doubt your ability.

A growth mindset is the belief that abilities, intelligence, and talents can be developed through dedication, effort, and perseverance. Coined by psychologist Carol Dweck, this concept contrasts with a fixed mindset, where individuals see their traits as unchangeable. Maintaining a growth mindset requires self-awareness, resilience, and a willingness to learn from failure.

This chapter will explore the key principles of a growth mindset, the barriers that often stand in the way, and practical strategies to cultivate and sustain it in various aspects of life. Because, in the end, *keeping a growth mindset isn't just about achieving a single goal—it's the foundation for lifelong success.* Those who embrace continuous learning, resilience, and adaptability will find that every challenge becomes an opportunity and every setback a lesson.

The Foundations of a Growth Mindset

① Understanding the Brain's Ability to Grow

Neuroscience research has demonstrated that the brain is malleable and capable of forming new neural connections through experience and practice. This concept, known as neuroplasticity, provides scientific support for a growth mindset. When we challenge ourselves, we strengthen neural pathways, improving our ability to learn and adapt.

② Effort Over Talent

A growth mindset prioritizes effort and persistence over innate talent. While talent may provide an initial advantage, it is a consistent effort that determines long-term success. Those with a growth mindset embrace challenges as opportunities to improve, rather than fearing failure.

③ Embracing Failure as a Learning Tool

Failure is not a sign of incompetence but a stepping stone toward mastery. Every setback provides valuable lessons that can lead to future improvements. Individuals with a growth mindset view mistakes as opportunities for growth rather than as personal shortcomings.

Overcoming Barriers to a Growth Mindset

Despite its benefits, many people struggle to maintain a growth mindset due to societal expectations, self-doubt, and past experiences. Identifying and addressing these barriers is crucial to sustaining a mindset of continuous improvement.

① **Fear of Failure**

One of the greatest obstacles to a growth mindset is the fear of failure. Many people avoid challenges because they are afraid of looking incompetent or being judged by others. Overcoming this fear involves reframing failure as a natural part of learning and progress.

② **Fixed Mindset Triggers**

Even individuals who typically have a growth mindset can experience fixed mindset triggers—situations that cause them to doubt their abilities. Common triggers include facing failure, facing competition, or struggling with a difficult task. Recognizing these moments and consciously shifting perspectives can help maintain a growth-oriented approach.

③ **Negative Self-Talk**

The way we talk to ourselves influences our mindset. Negative self-talk, such as "I'm not smart enough" or "I'll never get better at this," reinforces limiting beliefs. Replacing these thoughts with positive affirmations like "I can improve with practice" fosters resilience and motivation.

Strategies to Cultivate a Growth Mindset

① **Emphasize the Power of "Yet"**

Adding the word "yet" to negative statements can shift perception from limitation to possibility. Instead of saying, "I can't do this," saying, "I can't do this yet" reinforces the idea that improvement is possible with effort and time.

② **Set Process-Oriented Goals**

Rather than focusing solely on outcome-based goals, such as winning a competition or getting a promotion, individuals with a growth mindset set process-oriented goals. These goals focus on continuous learning and improvement, such as "I will practice this skill for 30 minutes each day."

③ Develop a Love for Learning

A commitment to lifelong learning is a hallmark of a growth mindset. Engaging in new challenges, exploring different perspectives, and staying curious fosters intellectual and personal growth. Reading books, taking courses, and seeking mentorship can all contribute to continuous learning.

④ Surround Yourself with Growth-Minded Individuals

The people we interact with influence our mindset. Surrounding oneself with individuals who value perseverance, learning, and resilience creates a supportive environment for personal and professional development.

⑤ Reframe Challenges as Opportunities

Instead of seeing challenges as threats, those with a growth mindset view them as opportunities for growth. Each difficulty presents a chance to develop new skills, gain experience, and strengthen resilience.

Applying a Growth Mindset in Different Areas of Life

① Education and Career

In academic and professional settings, a growth mindset is essential for continuous improvement. Students who believe intelligence can be developed are more likely to embrace challenges and persist through difficulties. In the workplace, professionals with a growth mindset seek opportunities for learning and are more adaptable to change.

② Relationships and Personal Development

A growth mindset extends beyond academics and careers—it plays a significant role in personal relationships.

Viewing conflicts as opportunities to improve communication and understanding strengthens relationships. Additionally, self-improvement through reflection and learning fosters personal growth.

③ Health and Well-being

A growth mindset is crucial in maintaining physical and mental well-being. Those who believe they can improve their health through effort are more likely to adopt healthier habits, such as exercising, eating well, and managing stress effectively.

④ Leadership and Teamwork

Leaders who embody a growth mindset inspire and empower others. They encourage their teams to take risks, learn from failures, and continuously develop their skills. In team settings, a growth mindset fosters collaboration and innovation.

The Long-Term Benefits of a Growth Mindset

Maintaining a growth mindset offers long-term advantages, including:

- **Increased resilience**: The ability to bounce back from setbacks and view challenges as learning experiences.
- **Higher motivation**: A focus on improvement rather than perfection leads to greater motivation and persistence.
- **Greater adaptability**: A willingness to learn and evolve makes it easier to navigate change and uncertainty.
- **Enhanced creativity**: An openness to new ideas and approaches fosters innovation and problem-solving skills.
- **More fulfilling experiences**: Embracing growth leads to a richer, more meaningful life.

In conclusion, a growth mindset is not a trait one is simply born with—it is a perspective that can be cultivated through conscious effort and practice. By embracing challenges, learning from failures, and maintaining a commitment to self-improvement, anyone can develop and sustain a growth mindset. The journey toward lifelong learning and personal growth is ongoing, but the rewards are immeasurable. When we shift our focus from fixed limitations to endless possibilities, we unlock our full potential and create a life of continuous progress and success.

Remember: *You are not only capable of reaching for the stars, but you can also touch them, too.*

I am rooting for you!

ABOUT JESSICA C. PHILLIPS

USA

Jessica C. Phillips is a dedicated martial arts practitioner who has achieved first-degree black belt rank since starting her training in 2019 under the guidance of her instructor, Hanshi Jessie Bowen. What started as a way to add a physical component to her fitness routine has turned into a journey of growth and healing. She's only beginning and plans to continue her studies and personal development journey. Her martial arts awards include placing #1 in Open Hand Kata in her first tournament in March 2022 and #2 in Open Hand Kata, Weapons Kata, and Sparring in March 2023.

In addition to her martial arts practice, Jessica is a Christian Minister, Mentor, Award-winning Author, and Magazine Columnist. She has written books such as *Be D.O.P.E.: Be Dependent on Prayer Every Day, Volumes I and II*, and has co-authored six books. Her academic achievements include being inducted into prestigious honor societies such as Phi Theta Kappa and the National

Society of Leadership and Success. In 2022, Jessica received the Presidential Community Service Lifetime Achievement Award, signed by President Joe Biden.

Jessica believes in the power of her words and only speaks greatness into her life and the lives of others. Additionally, she believes that she is not only capable of reaching for the stars, but through Christ, she can touch them, too. By sharing her experiences and insights, she hopes to inspire others to do the same.

FOR MORE INFORMATION:
- Website: bit.ly/JessicaCarollynAuthor
- LinkedIn: www.linkedin.com/in/phillips-jessica-c/

CHAPTER SIX

SECRETS TO LIFE: THE POWER OF THREE

BY ROCCI TWITCHELL

In many aspects of life, including martial arts, business, and our personal relationships, we often face life's challenges. We are not well equipped to handle the stresses and struggles that we are experiencing within those categories.

Martial arts training has taught me about "*The Power of Three.*" Martial arts training has also helped me understand and prepare for challenges.

The numerical value of three is significant within many forms of martial arts. In Filipino martial arts, the number three represents many different factors and concepts. Studying Filipino martial arts has greatly influenced the development of my martial arts career. In my T5 Boxing curriculum, we find The Power of Three.

Speed, Power, and Agility

A good boxer develops speed to help their ability to hit their opponent in the available target areas. Speed also helps build points and is useful for controlling and managing counterattacks.

Unfortunately, many boxers hide weaknesses and inability within speed, so speed alone has limitations. When boxing, it is also beneficial to have power and know when to use that power. Learning to harness power is an essential skill. Power should be used strategically and used to control and manipulate your opponent, if necessary. Power, of course, is used to knock out your opponent. Unfortunately, if power is overused, it can slow you down or even exhaust you and keep you from throwing meaningful and effective punches.

Speed and power are great tools, but a boxer is useless without agility. Boxers need the ability to move when punching with speed and power. Agility also keeps you from being counter-punched.

Footwork, Loop Shearing, and Compacting

In the art of Batu Pencak Silat, The Power of Three is essential. Footwork: Good footwork in Batu Pencak Silat creates the advantage you need for a confrontation. Knowing when to advance, step to the side, or retreat. The placement of footwork required in a confrontation is essential. Staying on your toes, moving to a flat-footed position using your heel, or placing your foot on the outside of your opponent's leg. All important functions for maneuvers with your feet and the upper body. Loop Shearing consists of maneuvers that keep your opponent's legs and upper arms trapped and unable to respond effectively. Circling and shearing your opponent's upper body and lower quadrant, keeping them from moving, is vital. Compacting is done when you have your opponent's legs and upper torso locked or jammed, and you drive them into the ground, making them unable to respond to your attack. Batu Pencak Silat is the ability to represent fluid body movements and keep your opponent from engaging you. Batu Pencak Silat was formed over many years of training with many Pencak Silat instructors. Back in 1995, my greatest inspiration, mentor, and instructor, Larry Hartsell, told me I would find the art of Silat amazing; he was right. My favorite instructor is Rita Suwanda from Mande Muda Pencak Silat.

Martial arts is a great way to find the secrets to life within business and your personal life. Most martial arts gyms have others seeking the secrets to life. Someone within your circle is looking, reading, and studying material to improve, learn, and grow. You can find that person over time and improve your skills. Find a person who likes to read motivational books or books on self-improvement. Guaranteed, you can find someone who wants to grow, improve, and learn within your martial arts community.

The Father, The Son, and The Holy Spirit

In my personal experience, I've found you can also find the secrets to life through The Father, The Son, and the Holy Spirit. Seeking the Lord's guidance has always been a positive and powerful tool in my life. Seeking a higher spiritual power for guidance has never been a negative aspect for me. Seeking a spiritual mentor helps you gain personal insight and understanding. Tibetan Monks come to Northern California annually to share their culture, traditions, and fantastic music. The many ways they approach life are unique and highly spiritual. I have a Tibetan Singing Bowl I carry in my backpack, and I play it often when I feel down or feel depressed, or overwhelmed by life's events. There are many different ways to find a spiritual connection. Finding a martial arts instructor who is humble, knowledgeable, and passionate about learning is extremely important. In the martial arts realm, we often find ourselves and instructors who have obtained rank or leadership skills that have grown stagnant and have become increasingly difficult to associate with. There is nothing worse than training with someone who knows everything and thinks they can't learn anymore.

Egos, Leadership & Rust

Egos, Leadership, Rust: these three do not make good decisions and don't create a healthy martial arts team.

Egos surround us in the workforce, at sporting events, and, unfortunately, in martial arts communities. Egos are difficult to deal with, dangerous, and destructive. Pure poison and evil. The ego is the enemy. A true leader is a person who is humble, wise, and has no ego. Leadership is the universal understanding that we all need to grow and thrive in a non-abusive manner and see the needs of all those on the team!

Rust is that other poison that eats at our brain and keeps our body idle, giving us a false sense of security. Rust can destroy relationships and destroy friendships. Rust is that small thought about giving up; rust can also be the small thought about cheating, lying, or giving up a few moral principles. Sometimes, "all that shines turns to rust." Don't be that person that loses their luster. Don't lose your shine; stay strong, focused, active, positive, and uplifting scenarios! Keep shining bright and make good choices in life.

In my personal experience as a bouncer, I found people gave into small trivial things that turned into large trivial circumstances, which turned into jail or a quick trip to the hospital, just because they didn't like the way I handled the chaotic alcohol-infused situation. Many times, I would offer a person three things. *"Get hurt, go to jail, a quick visit to the emergency room."* Three choices. Three principles. Sometimes, life has three choices.

Choose wisely!!

ABOUT ROCCI TWITCHELL

USA

I began my martial arts journey in 1982. In 1998, I started training with Larry Hartsell. Then, I started training with Guro Dan Inosanto in 2005. My Pencak Silat training began in 1995. My martial arts journey has continuously allowed me to meet great instructors and mentors and has kept me safe throughout my entire journey.

FOR MORE INFORMATION:
- Liahona Warrior Arts/T5-Boxing
- Email: rrtwitchell@me.com
- X: @rockytwitchell
- LinkedIn: @rocky-r-twitchell-a6996412
- Instagram: @rockinrandalltwitchell
- Facebook: @randall.twichell.3

SECRETS TO

LEADERSHIP

CHAPTER SEVEN

CHOSEN TO LEAD

BY JESSIE BOWEN

My story begins years before I ever considered myself a leader. As a child, I was bullied, told by teachers that I would never succeed, and rejected by sports teams because I was awkward and clumsy. There was no one who believed in me, and I struggled with finding my place in the world. I remember feeling invisible in a sea of more confident and capable children. But as I look back now, some 50 years later, I can clearly see how God had placed me exactly where I needed to be, allowing me to learn and grow into the leader I would eventually become.

I was not born with natural talents or charisma. In fact, I lacked the confidence and belief in myself that many others seemed to have. But God had a plan for me, one that would unfold over time. My journey into leadership truly began when I met someone who would change the course of my life: my martial arts instructor, O'Sensei Jan Wellendorf, the founder of Karate International of North Carolina.

At the time, I was tired of being picked on, called a coward, and feeling like I couldn't stand up for myself. Martial arts seemed like the answer. It wasn't just about defending myself physically; it was about finding a way to build my confidence, my strength, and my character. Little did I know, this path would lead me to a place I never imagined I would be—leading others.

O'Sensei Wellendorf was the first person who ever told me that I was good at something. He saw something in me that I could not see in myself. He taught me about the importance of setting goals, the power of persistence, and the value of discipline. Martial arts, in many ways, was a crucible for my personal development. It forced me to confront my fears, push past my limitations, and discover abilities I never thought I had. Through martial arts, I learned that leadership isn't about being perfect or without flaws; it's about having the courage to step forward and lead, even when you feel unprepared.

As I progressed through the ranks in martial arts, I was given more and more responsibilities. But there was one particular moment that stands out as a defining point in my journey as a leader. I will never forget the first time I was asked to lead a martial arts class. I stood there, facing 25 students who looked up to me, waiting for me to speak. In that moment, I was frozen. No words could come to mind. My heart raced, my hands trembled, and I felt like the biggest imposter. I quickly asked someone else to take over the class, excusing myself to retreat to my instructor's office.

When I walked into O'Sensei Wellendorf's office, he was sitting there, waiting for me. I had my head down, unable to meet his gaze, and I simply said, "Sir, I can't do this." He looked at me, almost as though he knew exactly what I needed to hear. Without hesitation, he responded, "Yes, you can. Take this book, go home, read it, and come back tomorrow." I took the book, feeling a bit defeated but also determined to figure out how to overcome this fear. I went home, read the book, and returned the next day, still nervous but now with a little more knowledge in my back pocket.

But when I stood in front of the class again, it wasn't much better. My nerves were still there, and I struggled to find my voice. Yet, something had shifted within me. I was no longer looking at the students as a source of judgment or pressure. Instead, I began to see them as people I was entrusted to guide. I still wasn't perfect, but I was learning to trust myself. I realized that leadership wasn't about being flawless—it was about showing up, being vulnerable, and learning along the way.

That day marked the beginning of my understanding of leadership. Leadership isn't just about having authority or making decisions; it's about showing up when it's hard, taking risks, and being willing to fail in order to grow. A leader is someone who is willing to step into the unknown, to take on challenges, and to inspire others to do the same.

As I advanced in rank, eventually earning my black belt, I began to fully embrace the role of a leader. My confidence grew as I applied the principles I had learned in martial arts: discipline, perseverance, and goal-setting. Leadership, I discovered, is not just about guiding others—it's about continuously growing and pushing yourself to become a better version of who you are. And in martial arts, the journey of self-improvement is never-ending.

After earning my black belt, I took on more leadership roles within the martial arts community. I became a teacher, a mentor, and a coach to others. I founded Karate International of Durham and built it into a thriving school, a place where students could not only learn martial arts but also grow as individuals. I realized that leadership wasn't confined to the dojo; it extended into every area of life.

In addition to martial arts, I also worked as a physical education instructor at Duke University and as a corporate educator at Duke Corporate Education. These experiences further deepened my understanding of leadership. In each role, I was entrusted with guiding others to achieve their full potential. Whether I was teaching students at the university, coaching athletes, or mentoring business professionals, I learned that the principles of leadership remain the same.

True leadership is about understanding people, building trust, and fostering an environment where others can succeed. It's about leading by example, even when no one is watching. It's about recognizing that everyone has the potential to be a leader, and your role is to help them realize that potential within themselves.

Throughout my life, I have learned that leadership is not a destination—it's a journey. It's a process of continuous learning, adapting, and growing. It's about stepping into uncomfortable situations, embracing challenges, and developing the courage to lead when it's not easy.

As I look back on my life, I realize that every challenge, every failure, and every moment of doubt was a stepping stone to the leader I am today. Being bullied as a child, being told I would never succeed—those experiences didn't define me. Instead, they served as the foundation for my growth. They taught me empathy, resilience, and the importance of believing in others when they don't believe in themselves. And, most importantly, they taught me that anyone, regardless of their background or circumstances, can rise to become a leader.

Again, leadership is not about being perfect. It's about being authentic, vulnerable, and willing to learn. It's about understanding that we all have the potential to lead, to inspire, and to make a difference in the lives of others. If I, a bullied child with no confidence or belief in myself, can rise to become a leader, then anyone can.

Today, as I look around at the students in my dojo and the individuals I mentor, I see the next generation of leaders. I see the same qualities in them that I once saw in myself: determination, perseverance, and the desire to grow. It's my mission now to pass on the lessons I've learned, to encourage them to step into their own leadership roles, and to remind them that leadership is about showing up, being present, and making a difference.

Being a leader is not about having the loudest voice or the most power—it's about serving others, lifting them up, and guiding them to realize their full potential. It's about making the world a better place, one step at a time, one person at a time. Leadership is a calling, and it is a privilege to answer that call. I am grateful for the journey I've been on, and I am honored to continue serving as a leader in whatever capacity God calls me to.

As I reflect on my journey, I realize that leadership is not just about personal growth but about the responsibility to guide and uplift others. The lessons I've learned—through challenges, mentorship, and perseverance—have shaped my understanding of what it truly means to lead. Leadership is not about seeking a title or position; it is about stepping forward, embracing challenges, and making a meaningful impact on those around us.

With that in mind, here are some additional important truths about leadership that I have come to understand over the years:

- **Leadership is a Continuous Journey**

  Leadership is not a destination but an ongoing process of growth, refinement, and service. Every challenge and triumph adds another layer to the foundation of a leader. True leadership is measured not by personal achievements but by the impact left on others.

- **True Leaders Focus on Impact, Not Recognition**

  The most meaningful measure of leadership is not in accolades or titles but in the lives touched and the people empowered. A leader's true legacy is seen in the students they train, the individuals they mentor, and the communities they serve.

- **Leadership is About Empowering Others**

  Great leaders do not seek to be the strongest or the most knowledgeable but instead focus on uplifting those around them. A leader's role is to help others recognize their potential, to provide encouragement, and to create opportunities for growth.

- **Perseverance Defines Leadership**

  Challenges and moments of doubt are inevitable, but true leadership is demonstrated in the decision to keep moving forward. Leaders must remain steadfast in adversity, pushing through uncertainty and obstacles with resilience and determination.

- **A Leader's Strength is in Inspiring Others to Lead**

  Leadership is not about gaining followers but about creating more leaders. The most effective leaders cultivate leadership in others, instilling principles of discipline, integrity, and courage so that those they mentor can step into their own leadership roles.

- **Leadership is About Connection, Not Isolation**

  While leadership sometimes requires making difficult decisions alone, true leadership is built on relationships. A strong leader fosters trust, builds community, and creates an environment where people feel valued and supported.

- **Adaptability is Key to Leadership**

  A leader must be willing to evolve, embrace new challenges, and continue learning. The ability to adapt to changing circumstances is essential for guiding others effectively and ensuring long-term success.

- **Leaders Must Have Vision**

  Effective leadership requires the ability to see beyond the present moment and inspire others to strive for a greater purpose. Leaders must help others recognize possibilities beyond their perceived limitations and encourage them to push toward excellence.

- **Leadership is Rooted in Responsibility, Not Power**

  Leadership is not about authority or prestige—it is about responsibility. It requires stepping up when needed, serving others with humility, and being willing to make difficult choices that align with a greater purpose.

- **Leadership Transforms Both the Leader and Others**

  The journey of leadership is one of continuous growth. By embracing leadership, individuals not only change the lives of those around them but also transform themselves, becoming stronger, more compassionate, and more purpose-driven.

Now, I challenge you to reflect on your own leadership journey. Where can you step up? Who can you inspire? How can you make a difference? You were chosen to lead—not by chance, but because your experiences, challenges, and lessons have prepared you for this moment. Leadership is not just about what you accomplish today; it's about the legacy you leave behind. Every decision you make, every person you mentor, and every life you touch becomes a part of your lasting impact. Whether in your family, workplace, dojo, or community, your leadership has the power to shape the future. Embrace the challenges, invest in others, and commit to building a legacy that will inspire generations to come. You were not just meant to follow the path—you were chosen to create it.

Now, step forward and lead.

ABOUT JESSIE BOWEN, PHD.

USA

Jessie Bowen is a 10-degree black belt, a two-time International Impact Award winner in biography publishing, and a bestselling author with over 30 books and audio programs on success, mindset, and personal development. As President of Elite Publications, he has helped countless authors publish and market their books, building credibility and influence in their industries.

A leader in independent publishing and media innovation, Jessie is the founder of the American Martial Arts Alliance Foundation and Institute, developing programs that elevate martial artists and entrepreneurs. His expertise in book marketing, branding, and author coaching has made him a sought-after authority in the publishing world.

His works include *Law of Attraction: Your Thoughts Determine Your Destiny*, *Unstoppable Confidence*, and *Change Your Mind, Change Your Life*. A former Duke University educator and Silva Method lecturer, Jessie blends goal-setting, mental performance, and martial arts principles to empower individuals and organizations.

Through Elite Publications and his author coaching programs, Jessie Bowen continues to help authors turn their stories into legacies, using publishing as a powerful tool for business growth and personal success.

FOR MORE INFORMATION:

American Martial Arts Alliance Foundation
- Website: www.whoswhointhemartialarts.com
- Email: amaawhoswho@gmail.com
- Instagram: @amaafoundation
- Facebook: @AMAAFoundation

Elite Publications
- Website: www.elitepublications.org
- Email: info@elitepublications.org
- Instagram: @elitepublications
- Facebook: @ElitePublicationsForAuthors

CHAPTER EIGHT

LEADERSHIP SECRETS

BY JAMES DEBROW III

The first act of accepting a leadership role is a personal one. For this reason, the personality of the leader is an important viable (Dulewicz & Higgs, 2005). It appears that many researchers have ignored cognition and knowledge as a factor (Bhat, 2002).

Knowledge is having possession of information and the ability to locate it. But cognition is something altogether different from knowledge and both are important (Ferraro, 1995); Debrow, 2012). Knowledge comes from the process of being educated. Cognition is the process of acquiring and basically understanding knowledge through applying thought, experiences, and by our senses, etc. Our senses are the building blocks for learning.

Leadership secrets are knowledge, experiences, energy, etc. Energy is critical to leadership because it can be transferred to others who are exhausted and stagnant. Leaders must be active. In the present (2024) postindustrial world, knowledge and energy are a leader's most prized possession (Bhat, 2002). Competition is fierce in this global experience market; leadership demands for our future existence are vitally important.

Even though a consensus definition of leadership is difficult, an agreed definition of knowledge is comprised of ideas, rules, procedures, information, cognition, and professional intellect, which all are essential for guiding people (Bhat, 2002).

More broadly, a qualitative longitudinal study presented four effective leadership traits: 1) behavioral, 2) cognitive, 3) personality, and 4) learning factors (Dulewicz & Higgs, 2005).

Whether you are operating a large entity or martial arts school, it will require a multitude of traits to be within the leader's wheelhouse, which will expose the leader's weakness if the traits are absent from their mental prowess.

In reviewing the previous work of Summerfield (2014) who cited Marie Kane's definition of leadership as, "taking people to places they've never been before (Ibid. p. 251)." Einstein's eleven test of leadership is simplistic, "If you can't explain it to a six-year-old, you don't understand it yourself (Ibid. p. 252)."

Leaders are trust builders in creating relationships where people feel secure, high reliability, honesty, and consistency between you and the teams. It is the relationship foundation that helps people to be vulnerable and open with others. "No matter what you do in life, relationships are currency (Pegues, 2021, P. 29)." One major strategy for fostering trust is to be clear, and consistent in communications (Savage, 2021).

Key aspects of leadership as defined by Covey (2004) are, "communicating to people their worth and potential so clearly that they come to see it in themselves (Ibid. p. 98)." Leadership is a professional obligation that requires a proper mindset to achieve greatness.

A descriptive definition pointed out by Terry (2021) is, "1) the act of leading a group of people or an organization; 2) the state or position of being a leader; and 3) the leaders of an organization or country (Ibid. P. 5)."

Dr. Jessie Bowen (2024), author and publisher identified three vital areas needed in a leader, "1) having a solid mindset focused on growth, 2) determination, and 3) resilience (Ibid. p. 198)." What is a growth mindset? Growth mindset is an individual's prowess to continue improving and learning through the vicissitudes of an organization. Crisis or chaos will continue to occur, and leaders must recover, adjust, change, and be flexible.

Fixed growth is the pathway to failure and is static. Fixed growth individuals espouse that intellect can only remain the same. Fixed growth people believe that talent by itself leads to success without great effort. Additionally, fixed growth persons do not take criticism well and tend to blame others for their failures. A growth mindset is better.

Leadership is the way in which a coach, for example, motivates others and typically provides direction (Predoiu, Makarowski, Görner, Bota, Predoiu, Mitrache, & Grigore, V., 2020, p. 129). Leaders must acquire social skills to be able to direct others (Brooks, 2023; Terry, 2021).

Researchers have reported many qualities of great leaders. Generally, strong character is a leadership quality but strong character by itself is insufficient (McRaven, 2023). It is imperative that leaders have leadership qualities in their own personal affairs to be able to transfer them to the professional arena. Professional actions are needed to, "plan; communicate intent; inspect the progress; hold people accountable; and that includes the leader too (Ibid. p. xvi)."

Combined actions and qualities are the substances that build great leaders. Any leader whose self-core-values are missing, e.g., character, will be reflected in the culture of an organization.

The lack of character will set new generations up for a doomsday event (McRaven, 2023). Character and integrity are paramount to ensure that the culture of an organization always puts doing things right in front of everything.

Motivation is the key to moving people from the comfortable state of mediocrity to a state of receptivity, e.g., from good to great because good is the enemy of great (Collins, 2001). Most times mediocrity means breaking through acts of favoritism and nepotism (Ibid. p. 31).

Oberdorfer (2024) quoted Sinek as saying that, "great leaders are the ones who think beyond 'short term' versus 'long-term,' because the landscape is rapidly shifting (Ibid, p. 46)." There are groundbreaking invocations almost daily.

There are predictive indications that suggest that leadership is vital for innovation management and the leader's decisive role is to improve creativity (Kesting, Uilhoi, Song & Niu, 2015). Leaders who are peak performers promote creativity and innovation in their cadre.

Leadership's lowest common denominator is having a clear vision to inspire people to achieve the eventual outcome of success (Collins & Zazier, 2020). Leaders do not make excuses about the lack of resources; instead, they utilize their selective processes more efficiently (Collins, 2005).

Understanding leadership begins with an understanding that the leader is only "one" and the number "one" is too small of a number to achieve greatness

(Maxwell, 2001). By Maxwell's (2001) calculation it is a myth to think that the "one person" can do it alone.

Schools of thought have consistently cited the criticality of teams and teamwork. It is an illusion that "one" leader thinks that they can walk alone in a leadership endeavor and be successful, let alone be great. Employees or students "buy-in" is essential for the sake of team concepts.

From Debrow's perspective, that would be naiveté and fruitless to go at it alone void of a divine calling. The two biggest hurdles of leadership are to create change and facilitate growth (Maxwell, 2011, p. 4). There are always societal changes as we change and grow toward decency (Ryan, 2024). People are dug into their proverbial holes and are comfortable there. These types of holes or known as silos and silos operate independently; and they must be controlled.

Silos, or hole systems, have a unique application in privilege information sharing only. Teams that work in their own holes or silos operate in isolation effecting effectiveness, efficiency, efficacy, innovation, and creative in an organization. Silos are a mentality that can restrict organizational growth. The way to defeat silos are to build stronger teams and collaborative relationships with all teams, and departments.

Notwithstanding, setting high expectations is vital to make the high standards clear to the students, employees, and the public at large (Krasnoff, 2015). Krasnoff (2015) cited a quote in a 2004 research project of Leithwood, Louis, Anderson, & Wahlstrom as follows, "There are virtually no documented instances of troubled schools being turned around without intervention by a powerful leader (Ibid. p. 3)." Leadership is crucial. The figure 4-I chart is a great start toward winning. *(see figure 4-I)*

(Collins & Zazier, 2020, p. 91). Be 2.0. Diagram of Vision, Strategy, Tactics. **Figure 4-I.**	
Vision ↓	**Core Values and Beliefs ↓** **Purpose ↓** **Mission ↓**
Strategy ↓	**Strategy ↓**
Tactics	**Tactics**

Pygmalion Effect or the Rosenthal Effect argues that it is an extraordinary psychological occurrence or phenomenon wherein the utilization of setting high expectations can lead to improved performance levels in each task area to create self-fulfilling prophecies. The prerequisite to the success of an organization is to set high standards.

The Pygmalion Effect is also known as, "Expectancy Theory, or Self-fulfilling Prophecies (Covey, 1989)." Leaders propound the idea to set high standards. Setting high expectations is the result of that expected behavior. High expectations lead to high performance and low expectations lead to low performance.

The importance of the Pygmalion Effect on topics related to the fact that children or students and employees will rise to what is expected of them, when coupled with treating the students or employees like they can achieve the task.

Setting high standards is the motivation needed to achieve greatness. Conversely, the anti-Pygmalion Effect in the educational domain has identified that the negative and phenomenal cases yielded, "you get what you expect, e.g., negative or positive results."

The duality of the Pygmalion Effect can be both positive or negative, but there are more factors besides the leader and teacher expectations, e.g., learner engagement, enthusiasm, student or employee motivation, influences, and achievement gains.

Positive teaching may or may not lead to student high achievements because of the many variables. Hence, setting high expectations is a prerequisite for productive results. The aim is to bring a positive attitude to set the altitude for students, employees, and teachers' growth for success.

The First-Tier executive leadership framework is concerned with performance management. Building a great organization requires performance metrics to be monitored to guide members back on track to the performance measures when needed (Eckerson, 2009).

Additionally, the performance rubrics must be accurate or there can be unintended issues. Unintended consequences of faulty metrics are: 1) loss in productivity, 2) unachievable goal setting losses, 3) demoralized employees, and 4) service losses.

Leadership and performance management's overarching criterion is to have a well-researched business plan. A business plan is a winning strategy to bring about a desired outcome. The business plan is the future of businesses that broach benchmarking, marketing strategies, identification of potential pitfalls, a guide for how to structure, and allocate needed resources.

The strategic planning process is vital to the success of an organization that entails a mission statement,

statement of values, core values, guiding principles, incentives, strategic mapping, etc. (Eckerson, 2009).

Strategic mapping will reveal the cause-and-effect connections to the strategic long-term objectives. Eckerson (2009) developed a wheel-model consisting of four parts: 1) strategizing, 2) planning, 3) monitoring the executed plan and making needed adjustments, and 4) act and adjust.

This study argues that half of knowledge is in the public sphere and the other half of knowledge is in the private sphere. Although an organization can monitor and control public knowledge, it finds it difficult to control private knowledge.

One way management can manage private knowledge is by creating an environment of collaboration and informal coordination. In so doing, an organization not only deepens its employees' knowledge base but also creates new organizational knowledge. Through participation and cooperation, an organization establishes a shared-schema to replace old knowledge with new knowledge that becomes necessary for continuous improvement and breakthrough innovations (Weick, 1995).

Yet, here are three very different leadership styles: 1) Autocratic leadership – this leadership model is where the leader's decisions are made alone void of a solution from the team; 2) Democratic (Participative) Leadership model – will consult with the team for decision-making; 3) Laissez-Faire Leadership – this leadership model provides little input and is a hands-off concept (Cartlin & Kemp, n.d.). Each style is applicable when used appropriately.

This chapter proposes that individual knowledge and organizational knowledge are distinct yet interdependent. Individual knowledge is often expressed through personal creativity and self-expression.

Organizational knowledge is reflected in products and services that an organization creates and sells to its customers. Individual expertise in an organization is an asset. But, if management does not nurture individual expertise carefully, individual self-expressions will become an organizational liability.

Accordingly, management should create an environment that encourages its employees to collaborate and share knowledge. This will result in improving an employee's knowledge base and create organizational knowledge through team interactions.

Leadership qualities are critical but leaders must control their own reactions also, and perceive their own actions; and how it affects external events (Predoiu, Makarowski, Görner, Bota, Predoiu, Mitrache, & Grigore, V., 2020). Leaders are always under the microscope.

In conclusion, leaders must master the art of being seen to a profound degree with great cunningness, skill, and subtlety (Brook, 2023). Conversely, leaders must master seeing others just as profoundly.

Being consistent is a positive leader goal (Martini, 2015). Our verbal and nonverbal communication must be fully aligned and congruent. Predictability and familiarity are considered two comfortable areas of a winning strategy.

Widely, leaders who are fair and consistent create a work environment where followers always know what is expected, no uncertainties, and fairness; and consistency is indoctrinated in an organization. Based on the fairness and consistency concepts, "leadership must abide by these rules themselves (Martini, 2015). There must not be any favoritism.

Most assuredly, ego, anxiety, and naivete are the recipe for low productivity. The leadership secrets are knowledge, studying great leaders, business plan, teambuilding, experience, communicating the leader's intent, and no excuses (Debrow, 2018).

"Ninety percent of all failures come from people who have a habit of making excuses – George Washington Carver – (McRaven, 2023, p. 174)."

Quote from Nelson Mandela – "Vision without action is just dream, action without a vision just passes time, and vision with action can change the world (Terry, 2021, p. 17)."

Executive Staff: James Debrow Fighting Tiger School, LLC., School of Champions: Dr. Clarence Montgomery, 10th Ju-Dan Red Belt, Counselor; Dr. Gregg Brown, 10th Ju-Dan Black Belt/Red Belt, Administrator; Dr. Derrick Whitlow I, 8th Dan/8th Level Black Sash; Dr. Robert Jackson, 7th Dan; Dr. John Williams, 7th Dan; Dr. James Clark, 7th Dan; Senior Instructor Derrick Whitlow II, 4th Dan.

References:

Sources held by the author.

ABOUT JAMES DEBROW III

USA

The Honorable James Von Debrow III is a Senior Law Enforcement Executive and retired Chief of Police in good standing, carrying the honorific and tactics title, "The Honorable." As a former chief of police, he was the head administrator of all police operations. The head administrator of police operations included senior executive command of the: police training academy, SWAT unit, patrol and detective units, internal affairs bureau, juvenile unit, jail facility, k-9 unit, narcotics unit, sex offenders' unit, dispatcher's communication unit, criminal analyst unit, bailiff's unit, motorcycle unit, records unit, administration unit, evidence and property room unit, fitness unit, and fleet unit.

Debrow is a retired Texas Department of Public Safety-State Troopers-Sergeant with twenty-five years of honorable and credible service. Former Sergeant James Debrow III was assigned to the Texas Department of Public Safety legendary Texas Highway Patrol Training

Bureau Staff. He developed and implemented the Bureau's law enforcement defensive full-contact karate-boxing-judo-jiu jitsu program.

James is a 10th Ju-Dan Red Belt and designated Federal and State Court-Certified Use-of-Force Expert by the judiciary; and President-Law Enforcement and Security Training Division for the United States Heads of Family Martial Arts Association, International Supreme Elite Warrior's Council.

FOR MORE INFORMATION:
- Email: policeexecutiveslei@yahoo.com
- Facebook: www.facebook.com/profile.php?id=100071560697609

CHAPTER NINE

THE SECRETS TO LEADERSHIP

BY LINDA DENLEY

Leadership is not something that happens overnight. It is a journey shaped by trials, discipline, and the drive to bring out the best in others. Over my lifetime, I've worn many hats—competitor, mentor, teacher, and, most importantly, leader. As a world martial arts champion, I've had the honor of leading students, peers, and even entire communities toward excellence. What I've learned through these experiences is that leadership is not about standing above others but walking alongside them. Let me share with you the secrets to leadership that I've come to live by.

① Lead by Example

When I stepped into the dojo for the first time, I was captivated by my instructor's presence. They didn't just tell us what to do—they showed us. They executed every kick, every punch, every bow with the kind of precision and respect that left no room for doubt. It was clear they lived by the very principles they taught. That stuck with me.

As I climbed the ranks in martial arts and became a teacher, I knew I had to do the same. If I expected my students to work hard, I had to work harder. If I wanted them to respect the art, I had to show unwavering respect in everything I did. Leadership is about setting the standard. I can't ask anyone to do what I'm not willing to do myself.

One of my proudest moments came not from winning championships but from watching my students win theirs. It was a reflection of the work we'd put in together. They followed because they knew I wouldn't ask for their best unless I gave them mine.

② Vision is the Anchor

Leadership without vision is like a ship without a compass. I've always believed that to lead effectively, you must have a clear idea of where you're going. Early in my career, I set a vision not just for myself but for the women in martial arts. In a sport dominated by men, I wanted to prove that women could not only compete but excel.

This vision wasn't just about me winning titles; it was about creating opportunities for others. I saw a future where young girls could walk into a dojo and see themselves reflected in their instructors, in the champions they idolized, and in the respect they earned.

A leader's vision is not always immediately understood or accepted. I faced plenty of resistance along the way. But when you hold onto your vision, others will begin to see it, too. Once they do, they'll rally around it. Today, I'm proud to see so many women thriving in martial arts, and I know that vision played a part in making it happen.

③ Resilience is the Bedrock

Let me tell you a secret: the path to leadership is not a smooth one. There were moments when I wanted to give up—times when the odds seemed stacked too high, the challenges too great. But here's what I learned: resilience is not just enduring adversity; it's growing because of it.

There was one tournament in particular that tested me. I walked in with high expectations, but I lost in the first round. The defeat was crushing. For a brief moment, I doubted myself as a competitor and a leader. But then I asked myself what kind of example I would be setting if I gave up now.

I went back to the dojo, trained harder than ever, and came back stronger. Months later, I won that same tournament. That victory meant more to me than any other because it wasn't just about skill—it was about resilience. As a leader, your ability to bounce back inspires others to do the same. People don't just follow your successes; they follow how you handle your failures.

④ Communication is the Key

Leadership is not a one-way street. If you want to inspire others, you have to connect with them. And that starts with communication. I learned early on that people won't follow you just because you have a title or a trophy. They'll follow you because you take the time to understand them and speak to their hearts.

In the dojo, every student is different. Some are confident and eager, while others are shy and unsure. My job as a leader is to meet them where they are and guide them forward. That means asking questions, listening to their concerns, and tailoring my teaching to their needs.

I remember one student who struggled with self-doubt. No matter how much I encouraged him, he couldn't see his potential. One day, instead of telling him what to do, I asked him, "Why do you think you're here?" What brought you to martial arts? His answer was raw and honest: he wanted to be strong for his family. From that moment, I shifted my approach, tying every lesson back to his deeper motivation. Over time, he transformed—not just as a martial artist but as a person.

Good leaders talk. Great leaders listen.

⑤ Empathy Makes a Difference

If there's one thing I've learned about leadership, it's that people will forget what you said or did, but they'll never forget how you made them feel. Leadership isn't about barking orders or being untouchable; it's about building trust and showing empathy.

I've had my share of tough students—those who resist authority, challenge every instruction and seem determined to test your patience. But I've learned that behind every tough exterior is a story. When you take the time to understand someone's struggles, you can lead them more effectively.

There was a young woman who joined my class after losing her father. She was angry, withdrawn, and hesitant to trust. Instead of pushing her to perform, I gave her space to heal, letting her take things at her own pace. Slowly, martial arts became her outlet, and she began to open up. Today, she's one of my most dedicated students, and she credits martial arts with helping her rebuild her confidence and strength.

Empathy is not a weakness; it's a leader's greatest strength.

⑥ Empowerment is Leadership

To me, the greatest measure of a leader is not how many people follow them, but how many leaders they create. True leadership is about empowering others to take the reins and shine in their own right.

I've always made it a point to give my students opportunities to step into leadership roles. Whether it's leading warm-ups, coaching younger students, or even teaching a class, these moments help them discover their own potential.

One of my former students is now a dojo owner, and nothing makes me prouder than seeing her inspire the next generation. She once told me, "You didn't just teach me martial arts; you taught me how to believe in myself." That, to me, is the essence of leadership—helping others see what they're capable of.

⑦ Discipline is the Foundation

If there's one thing martial arts has taught me, it's the value of discipline. Discipline is what keeps you going when motivation fades. It's what separates good leaders from great ones.

As a competitor, there were days when I didn't feel like training. I was tired, sore, and tempted to take a break. However, discipline reminded me of my goals and pushed me to keep going. The same principle applies to leadership. People are watching, and your consistency sets the tone.

Discipline isn't just about physical effort—it's about mental and emotional fortitude. It's about showing up, doing the work, and staying true to your values, even when it's hard. As a leader, you can't afford to take shortcuts. Your discipline inspires others to hold themselves to the same standard.

⑧ Adaptability is Crucial

If there's one thing life has taught me, it's that nothing stays the same. As a leader, you have to be adaptable. Situations change, people change, and your approach must evolve.

In sparring, no two opponents are alike. You have to adjust your strategy on the fly, anticipating their moves and finding new ways to counter them. Leadership works the same way. You can't rely on one-size-fits-all solutions. You have to be flexible, creative, and willing to learn.

When the pandemic hit, I had to adapt my teaching methods, moving classes online and finding new ways to engage my students. It was a challenge, but it also reminded me of the importance of resilience and innovation. As a leader, your ability to adapt inspires others to face change with confidence.

⑨ Leadership is Service

At its core, leadership is about serving others. It's about putting the needs of your team, your students, or your community above your own.

I've always believed that leadership is a privilege. It's not about power or recognition—it's about making a positive impact. Whether it's mentoring a struggling student, volunteering in the community, or promoting inclusivity in martial arts, I see every act of service as an opportunity to lead by example.

Leadership isn't about being in the spotlight; it's about shining that spotlight on others.

⑩ A Leader's Legacy

Finally, leadership is about legacy. It's not just about what you achieve but what you leave behind. I want my legacy to be more than titles and trophies. I want it to be the lives I've touched, the leaders I've mentored, and the barriers I've helped break.

Every time I see one of my students step onto the mat with confidence, I know my leadership has made a difference. Every time I hear from a young woman who says she was inspired to take up martial arts because of me, I feel that my vision is being fulfilled.

Leadership is not a destination; it's a journey.

ABOUT LINDA DENLEY

USA

Considered the G.O.A.T. of women's sport karate, Grand Master Linda Denley is an American karate champion who was born in Houston, Texas. She was rated number one in Sport Karate from 1973 to 1996. Her influence inspired a generation of women to compete in martial arts. Grand Master Linda Denley's legacy extends beyond the ring. Her impressive track record as both a fighter and a world-class coach trainer, coupled with her role as a professional school owner, places her at the pinnacle of martial arts expertise. Denley's influence reaches worldwide, evident in her positions on the Boards of Directors for prestigious martial arts organizations and her longstanding dedication to producing and promoting sports karate tournaments.

FOR MORE INFORMATION:

- Texas Black Belt Academy Houston
- Email: texasblackbeltacademyhouston@gmail.com
- Facebook: @GrandMasterLindaDenley

CHAPTER TEN

THE GOLD STANDARD

BY AL FARRIS

I want to start by expressing my honor in sharing my thoughts on life and the various secrets of leadership. The concepts of leadership and life are vast and open to interpretation, with each person having their own opinion and definition. There are numerous definitions regarding the secrets of leadership, each reflecting different perspectives on its true meaning. What are these secrets of leadership? Our world and cultures are continually evolving in many directions each day.

I believe you should always be yourself and surround yourself with positive, like-minded individuals. They should share your values, integrity, and professionalism. Let your moral compass point true north! This is true leadership.

It is important to understand what shapes a person's identity. Most would agree that this development is influenced by various factors, including parents, siblings, friends, neighbors, schools, faith, and personal experiences. All of these elements can significantly impact how a person grows and evolves. People can be influenced by both positive and negative experiences.

Most people will agree that the following traits should be an integral part of life:

- Live an authentic and honest life, embracing integrity.
- Lead a good, clean life and show care for others.
- Live in the moment; be present and engaged.
- Be genuine in your interactions with others.
- When someone is speaking, actively listen, understand, and communicate with them.
- Ensure that they feel their conversation is the most important thing in your life at that moment.
- Manage your time effectively, stay focused, and maintain a clear vision.
- Learn from your mistakes and the mistakes of others. Acknowledge them and move forward.
- Be grateful, kind, and show appreciation.
- Lead by example and embody true leadership.
- Maintain integrity and be above reproach.
- Help others whenever possible.
- Be honest, ethical, and moral; always speak the truth.
- Listen attentively when someone is sharing their feelings openly.
- Consider the consequences of major life decisions, as your choices can impact others. (Count your costs.)
- Avoid sharing negative comments or rumors; practice restraint.
- It's essential to listen intently to those around us.
- James 1:19 - Everyone should be quick to listen and slow to speak

It is important to think carefully before you speak and choose your words wisely. Once you speak, your words cannot be taken back. Therefore, consider your thoughts clearly before sharing them. The Bible often refers to the tongue as a double-edged sword, emphasizing its potential to either harm or uplift others. Our words hold great power and can impact people both positively and negatively.

My dad once asked me a question when I sought his advice: "*Have you counted the costs?*" Initially, I thought he was referring to money, but it turned out to be more profound. He was encouraging me to analyze all facets of the decision I faced and consider the potential effects it might have on my life. That moment became a significant turning point for me from a philosophical standpoint. I still apply this technique today, and it works extremely well for me.

I have always had a genuine desire to help others. I developed these values early in life. My core values and personal philosophy are to touch lives, change lives, and save lives!

I am known for my philosophy and core values, which include being ethical, moral, and legal. I value strong friendships, life coaching, mentorship, and leaving lasting impressions.

Your reputation, accomplishments, and drive will speak for themselves. Those who truly know you will highlight your integrity throughout your life's journey. People will learn who you are and what you stand for. For me, the essence of leadership is not about being financially wealthy; it's about being the best person I can be and making a difference in the lives of others. While money is necessary for survival, it is not everything. When my life is over, I want to be remembered for how I helped and treated others. None of us is perfect, but we should all strive for excellence.

A recipe for the secrets of leadership in life:

- Genuinely care about people and their well-being.
- Be kind.
- Communicate effectively with people at all levels.
- Be an attentive listener.
- Demonstrate confidence, enthusiasm, and passion.
- Be transparent and clear in your communication.
- Lead by example.
- Invest in yourself.
- Invest in your relationships.
- Understand and appreciate others.
- Take responsibility for your actions.
- Handle conflicts with grace.
- Learn from your failures and grow from them.
- Always do the right thing.
- Strive to set yourself apart from others.
- Possess and demonstrate integrity in all your actions.
- Practice compassion and show sympathy towards others.
- Avoid judging others; focus on your own journey.
- Recognize your limitations and work within them.
- Prioritize your family and children over the pursuit of money. (If you prioritize money over family, you may look back and regret choices you cannot change.)
- Maintain a healthy balance in life.
- Stay humble in your achievements.
- Strive to touch lives, change lives, and save lives!
- Being a strong leader can sometimes feel lonely, much like an eagle soaring high above the ground.
- Surround yourself with like-minded individuals for mutual growth and support.

Live an ethical, moral, and legal life. When faced with life's challenges or decisions, remain true to yourself and others.

Always let your moral compass guide you in the right direction.

Today, I hear people expressing uncertainty about the changes in life. They feel that what was once considered right is now viewed as wrong, and vice versa. Life will continue to evolve, and it's important to adapt. Serve your family, friends, community, and country to the best of your ability. Stay authentic and strive to help those around you.

I strive to help people reach their personal best and create a positive global impact. When I teach, lecture, or provide training, those around me can see my genuine passion for making a difference in their lives. They often compliment my analogies and the information I present, referring to it as "The Gold Standard." By sharing my methodologies and philosophies, I can effectively influence their lives from a unique perspective. I believe in treating everyone and everything with respect.

Touch Lives, Change Lives, and Save Lives!

ABOUT AL FARRIS

USA

Studying martial arts had a significant positive impact on Grandmaster Farris' life from an early age. When he began his career in law enforcement, he recognized a tremendous need for training in various martial arts disciplines. Grandmaster Farris understood that officers must be well-rounded in their skills. In fact, martial arts have saved his life on several occasions. Grandmaster Farris developed a unique system for emergency first responders, dedicating decades to studying, analyzing, and refining techniques that have proven effective. He incorporated self-defense strategies to contain, restrain, control, and submit violent individuals, creating a system tailored for today's warriors. This led to the establishment of the Modern Warrior System 360, which has saved many lives in both law enforcement and the community. The training he has provided during civil unrest, protests, and riots over the past several years has saved the lives of both officers and community members. Many have referred to him as the "Law Enforcement Officer of the

Decade." He has also contributed to the development of a nationwide program aimed at stopping active shooters. Grandmaster Farris is committed to helping people, and his philosophy is simple and direct: "*Touch Lives, Change Lives, and Save Lives!*"

FOR MORE INFORMATION:

- The Modern Warrior System 360
- Email: icgm@grandmasteral.com

CHAPTER ELEVEN

A GUIDE TO LEADERSHIP

BY THOMAS FLEMING

I was asked by Elite Publications to share my views on leadership, drawing from over 56 years of teaching karate, as well as the experiences and lessons I have learned along the way. Below is a list of what I believe a leader should embody. First, it is essential to understand what leadership entails. A leader should be disciplined, respectful, confident in their actions, and able to listen and respond with understanding rather than ego.

(1) A leader listens very carefully before responding. This involves not only hearing the question but also understanding what is being asked. After listening, it can be helpful to restate the question to the person you are speaking with. This shows that you have accurately heard them and allows you time to gather your thoughts before responding. Additionally, this approach reassures the individual that you value their input, as they appreciate that you took the time to listen and did not interrupt them while they expressed their views. Ultimately, it makes them feel heard and respected.

(2) A leader recognizes the potential in each student and supports them in achieving their goals rather than diminishing their confidence. As a leader, it is important to see each individual for who they are and to understand what they can learn or contribute. This involves identifying their strengths and weaknesses and building upon them

through positive feedback and encouragement. Negative criticism can destroy a student's confidence, cause them to lose face among peers, and ultimately lead to quitting. It's essential to foster a supportive environment that promotes growth and perseverance.

③ Leadership is not about you and your ego; it's about the goals of each student. Many instructors or leaders mistakenly believe that their value is linked to their students' success, thinking that the better their students perform, the better they will be perceived by the world, which boosts their egos. They often forget to focus on the students' actual needs and goals. Remember, your time in the spotlight has passed. Now it's time to share what you have learned so that your students can shine and have their own moment of success.

④ Effective leadership involves the ability to delegate tasks to your volunteers, kyu belts, and black belts in a way that makes them feel valued and proud of their contributions. It's important to reward your team by assigning them tasks that inspire or challenge them, helping to build their confidence. Additionally, always remember to compliment and thank them for their efforts. These small gestures can have a significant impact on your students.

⑤ Leadership is knowing how to resolve disputes in a way that doesn't have anyone lose face but resolves the dispute amicably for both parties. This requires taking the time to thoroughly understand the perspectives of each side. Look for common ground that both parties can agree on to facilitate resolution. If a decision must be made, it is often best to allow a few days for emotions to settle before revisiting the issue to find a cooperative path forward. This approach helps achieve a mutually satisfactory outcome.

⑥ Leadership is making the tough decisions that will come, and believe me they will come. At some point, you will be faced with a difficult choice that may not be pleasant for you or the students involved. For instance, if you learn that one of your students is bullying others and has caused harm, you may confront the student. If they show no remorse and exhibit a negative attitude, that presents a challenging situation. Now, you must make a hard decision: what do you do? Everyone may have a different answer, but ultimately, it is your decision to make. Once you make it, you must live with the consequences.

⑦ Leadership is not crossing the line but holding fast to your beliefs and expressing them to keep your standards high and not give into outside pressures that would lower your standards. It's essential not to succumb to external pressures that may compromise those standards. Throughout my years as president of the CKA, there have been attempts to persuade us to ease the grading process for Black Belts, such as using simpler grading sheets or reducing the requirements to earn a Black Belt. It is crucial never to lower your standards, as doing so would undermine the work of those who came before you and result in a loss of respect for you and your club or organization. Remember, people choose to come to you because of your reputation. Therefore, do not lower your standards.

⑧ Leadership is the highest level of self-discipline, it guides you every day in all your choices you make as you are an example to your students and community. It is important to be respectful, courteous, and helpful to everyone you meet in the community. Remember, one wrong move or harsh word can undo what took a lifetime to build.

⑨ Don't be afraid to embrace leadership, embrace it. You have a lot to offer based on what you've learned throughout your journey, and you are ready to pass that knowledge on to help others achieve their goals. Have confidence in your ability to succeed in anything you set your mind to.

⑩ Leadership is about continuous growth—learning new ideas, methods, and perspectives—and knowing how to introduce them to benefit your students.

⑪ There are no true secrets to leadership; it comes with experience and learning from your mistakes.

⑫ Authentic leadership involves listening and learning from those who have come before you, as they have much to offer. You can learn a great deal from their triumphs and failures if you take the time to listen and apply those lessons to your own journey. By heeding their advice and avoiding the mistakes they share, you can significantly enhance your development as a leader.

⑬ A leader is not afraid to ask questions or seek advice and counsel from others to aid in decision-making. What I want to emphasize is that everyone needs help along their journey, so don't hesitate to ask tough questions. If you can't find an answer or don't understand something, seek out someone who does and ask for their guidance.

⑭ Effective leadership involves recognizing your limitations and bringing people into your circle who can help you achieve your goals. Every good instructor is aware of their limitations and should collaborate with others in their group to enhance ideas and efforts, ultimately benefiting the knowledge and competency of their students and Black Belts. For example, inviting special guests like Bill Wallace to teach fighting techniques or hosting seminars with top Black Belts to instruct on kata or weapons is an excellent way to support your students in achieving their goals.

⑮ Leadership involves understanding the challenges each student faces and finding ways to support them—not just physically, but also emotionally. It's about instilling confidence, strength, and leadership skills in students so they can overcome their difficulties.

⑯ Effective leadership requires reflecting on your day to identify how to improve your lessons. You should consider whether you learned something new and whether your students benefited from what you taught. Leadership also means recognizing when a teaching method didn't work as planned and figuring out how to adjust it so that it effectively supports your students' learning.

⑰ Leadership involves discipline, confidence, and self-respect to successfully complete your tasks. It's important for leaders to believe in themselves and recognize that they are on the right track, committing to see through their plans and endeavors until they are satisfied with the outcomes.

⑱ A key aspect of leadership is being well-prepared. This means having all the necessary information organized for meetings or class events. The worst mistake a leader can make is arriving at a meeting or teaching a class unprepared, as this demonstrates incompetence to the group or class.

⑲ Leadership is about ensuring that no one is left out or feels excluded; there is no worse feeling than being left out. A good leader recognizes that students genuinely want to belong and be part of what is happening. Sometimes, they might be too shy or lack the confidence to express this desire, so it's important to reach out and ask them.

⑳ If you don't know something as a leader, remember to ask! Gather all the facts, verify that they are correct, and then take action based on that information.

In conclusion, leadership is not easy; it requires hard work and discipline. However, this effort can build your self-esteem and confidence, which will, in turn, be reflected in your interactions with others. When you stay true to your core values, the respect you earn as a true leader will be significant. Ultimately, no matter what you do in life, being a leader will be one of your most rewarding experiences.

I wish you all the best and good luck in your Leadership Journey!

ABOUT THOMAS FLEMING

CANADA

I began my journey in martial arts at the age of 9, starting with Judo at the YMCA. As time passed, I wanted to explore something different and discovered Karate under the instruction of Sensei George Sylvain and achieved the rank of Shodan through the Canadian Karate Association. When my instructor informed me that he was quitting Karate, I received the opportunity to train with Sensei Fern Cleroux, thanks to a letter of introduction from Sensei George Sylvain.

From that point on, I trained with the Cleroux Karate Club for over 50 years, and I still wear his crest today. Throughout the years, I participated in various competitions at regional, national, and international levels. Later, I became a Team Coach and eventually achieved the rank of Judan from the Canadian Karate Association Grading Board.

I opened my first club in Blossom Park, followed by locations in Carlsbad Springs, Winchester, Vernon,

Chesterville, Akwesasne, and Howick, Quebec. During this time, I also became a member of the Canadian Karate Association in 1972. Over the years, I progressed from a regular member to a club member, then to Vice President, and now I hold the position of President of the Canadian Karate Association.

FOR MORE INFORMATION:

- Fleming Karate Club
- Website: www.flemingkarateclub.com
- Email: fleming.karate@hotmail.com

CHAPTER TWELVE

MARTIAL ARTS: A FOUNDATION FOR LEADERSHIP & LIFELONG ACHIEVEMENT

BY JOHN KERECZ

The Foundation of Leadership and Lifetime Achievement Through Martial Arts: Lessons from Over 57 Years of Training

Martial arts is not just a physical discipline; it is a lifelong journey of personal growth, mental strength, and character development. Reflecting on more than 57 years of martial arts training, which began when I was six, I realize how this practice has established a foundation for leadership, goal-setting, and the perseverance to achieve those goals. The lessons I have learned on the mat, in the dojo, and through my interactions with mentors have profoundly influenced every aspect of my life. They shape my approach to challenges and guide how I inspire and support others.

The Early Years: Building Discipline and Resilience

At the age of six, I stepped into the world of martial arts under the tutelage of Shi-han Sensei Louis Casamassa, the

Great Grand Master of Red Dragon Karate. My initial exposure to martial arts was rooted in a blend of Judo, Karate, and Gung-Fu. These formative years were instrumental in instilling discipline, resilience, and the importance of perseverance.

As a child, I learned that progress is not achieved through talent alone but through consistent effort. The repetition of basic forms, dedication to perfecting techniques, and humility in accepting correction taught me that success is built brick by brick. I carried this understanding into my academic and personal life, realizing that goals—whether mastering a kata or excelling in school—require a clear vision and the discipline to work steadily toward them.

Setting and Achieving Goals: The Martial Arts Way

Martial arts is inherently goal-oriented. Whether it's earning belts or mastering techniques, there's always a tangible milestone to strive for. This structure helped me develop an early understanding of how to set achievable goals and break them down into manageable steps.

For example, earning a new belt wasn't just about passing a test; it involved daily practice, consistent improvement, and overcoming setbacks. This experience taught me how to tackle long-term goals in life. When I decided to pursue advanced education or start a challenging project, I approached it similarly to my practice in martial arts: by creating a roadmap, committing to daily progress, and staying resilient in the face of obstacles.

Leadership Lessons Learned on the Mat

Martial arts has placed me in environments where leadership was both modeled and required. My mentors, including Shi-han Sensei Casamassa and, later, figures like Soke Michael DePasquale Jr., exemplified essential leadership qualities such as integrity, empathy, and decisiveness. Observing how they guided others with patience and purpose inspired me to incorporate those traits into my own life.

As I advanced in rank and skill, I naturally took on leadership roles within the dojo. Teaching younger students, assisting with classes, and eventually mentoring others refined my ability to communicate effectively and inspire confidence. Leadership in martial arts isn't about asserting authority but about serving as a guide and role model. This principle has shaped how I lead in both professional and personal contexts, emphasizing collaboration, encouragement, and leading by example.

The Role of Mentorship in Leadership Development

Mentorship has been a fundamental part of my martial arts journey and has significantly shaped my approach to leadership. My mentors not only taught me techniques but also shared valuable life lessons, instilled important values, and encouraged me to reach my full potential. They emphasized the importance of supporting the growth of others and celebrating their successes as if they were my own.

As I transitioned into mentorship roles myself, I came to understand that effective leadership is about empowering others. Whether I am helping a student perfect their form or guiding a colleague through a complex project, my goal is to provide the tools and support they need, rather than simply giving instructions.

The Skills That Martial Arts Imparts

Throughout the decades, martial arts has provided a wealth of skills that have been instrumental in achieving my goals and leading effectively. Among these skills, the most significant include:

① Focus and Mindfulness

Martial arts demands unwavering focus, whether executing a precise technique or sparring with an opponent. This ability to concentrate fully on the task at hand has proven invaluable in all areas of my life. When facing challenges, I have learned to stay present, analyze the situation, and respond thoughtfully instead of reacting impulsively.

② Adaptability and Problem-Solving

No two sparring matches or training sessions are ever the same. Martial arts teaches you to adapt to new circumstances, anticipate your opponent's moves, and respond with creativity and strategy. This ability to adapt has been essential in navigating life's uncertainties and finding innovative solutions to various problems.

③ Emotional Regulation and Resilience

Martial arts is not only about mastering the body, but also about mastering the mind. Learning to remain calm under pressure, manage frustration, and recover from defeat has been one of the most valuable skills I've acquired. These lessons have prepared me to handle stressful situations in leadership roles with composure and confidence.

④ Goal-Setting and Time Management

Achieving martial arts milestones requires careful planning and consistent effort. Balancing training with other responsibilities taught me how to set priorities, manage my time effectively, and stay committed to long-term objectives.

⑤ Empathy and Teamwork

Training with partners cultivates a strong sense of empathy and collaboration. It teaches you to understand others' emotions, support their growth, and work together toward shared goals. This approach has been essential in building strong relationships and creating supportive teams in every aspect of my life.

⑥ Confidence and Self-Belief

Overcoming challenges in martial arts—whether it's breaking a board or sparring with a tougher opponent—instills a sense of confidence and self-belief that extends into every aspect of life. This inner strength has been a cornerstone of my leadership skills and has empowered me to pursue ambitious goals.

Applying Martial Arts Principles to Lifetime Achievement

The principles of martial arts have significantly shaped my personal development and provided a framework for achieving lifelong goals. For example, when I decided to pursue advanced ranks in multiple disciplines, including Hapkido, Kenpo, and Jujitsu, I drew on the goal-setting and perseverance skills that I developed during my early years of training.

Similarly, as I transitioned to promoting modern systems like Paxtial Arts under Ed Parker Jr., I utilized the adaptability and leadership skills I had learned through decades of practice. Embracing new ideas while respecting tradition has been crucial for remaining relevant and effective in a rapidly changing world.

The Role of Martial Arts in Leadership Roles

Martial arts has played a crucial role in my professional and community leadership experiences. The confidence, focus, and problem-solving skills I developed through training have empowered me to lead teams, mentor others, and effectively manage complex challenges.

For instance, as a mentor and ambassador for martial arts, I have utilized principles of empathy and collaboration to build strong relationships and inspire others to reach their full potential. Whether working with students in the dojo or guiding professionals in various fields, the lessons of martial arts have consistently served as my guiding principles.

Inspiring the Next Generation

One of the greatest rewards of my martial arts journey has been the opportunity to inspire and guide the next generation. Watching my students and their students grow, achieve their goals, and carry on the traditions of martial arts has been incredibly fulfilling.

I emphasize to my students that martial arts is not just about physical techniques; it is also about cultivating the skills and mindset needed to succeed in all areas of life. By instilling discipline, resilience, and a commitment to lifelong learning, I hope to empower them to become leaders in their own right.

Conclusion: A Lifetime of Growth Through Martial Arts

Reflecting on over 57 years of martial arts training, it's clear that the lessons learned in the dojo extend far beyond its walls. The discipline, focus, resilience, and leadership skills developed through martial arts have provided a solid foundation for achieving lifetime goals and inspiring others.

Martial arts is not just a practice; it is a way of life—a journey of constant growth and self-improvement. As I continue this journey, I remain committed to using the skills and values I have acquired to lead, mentor, and make a positive impact in the world. My hope is that by sharing these lessons, I can inspire others to embrace the transformative power of martial arts in their own lives.

ABOUT JOHN KERECZ

USA

Grand Master John Kerecz has over 57 years of martial arts experience. He began his journey in 1967 under the guidance of the late Shi-han Sensei Louis Casamassa, the Great Grand Master of Red Dragon Karate and the founder of the American Karate Kung Fu Federation (A.K.K.F.). Shi-han's dynamic teachings in Judo, Karate, and Gung-Fu provided Grand Master Kerecz with a solid and diverse foundation, sparking his lifelong dedication to martial arts.

Over the decades, Grand Master Kerecz has achieved high ranks in Hapkido, Kenpo, and Jujitsu while also exploring a variety of martial arts disciplines. This ongoing journey has deepened his understanding of the diverse traditions and techniques within martial arts. Currently, he serves as an Ambassador under Grand Master Ed Parker Jr., promoting Paxtial Arts—a modern martial arts system that combines tradition, innovation, and peaceful resolution strategies.

Grand Master Kerecz is not only focused on personal mastery but is also deeply committed to mentoring his students and supporting their extended martial arts lineage. His guidance promotes their growth, health, and success, ensuring that their traditions are preserved and evolved. His enduring dedication reflects not only his technical expertise but also his belief in martial arts as a path for lifelong learning, personal development, and community enrichment.

FOR MORE INFORMATION:

- KereKan Martial Arts
- Website: www.johnkerecz.com
- Email: Johnkerecz@outlook.com
- Facebook: www.facebook.com/john.kerecz?mibextid=LQQJ4d

CHAPTER THIRTEEN

EXECUTIVE LEADERSHIP IN MARTIAL ARTS: PRINCIPLES, CHALLENGES & STRATEGIES

BY DR. JEAN KFOURY

Introduction

Effective leadership is crucial for achieving organisational success, whether in martial arts schools or broader enterprises. Leaders must clearly articulate a vision and ensure the cohesive execution of strategies.

A leadership role resembles a woven tapestry, where various skills interlace to create a strong and effective leader. Together, these skills foster unity and strength.

Executive leaders aim to guide their team members and achieve the organisation's defined business goals. The role of an executive leader is becoming increasingly complex. Leaders must have a clear, defined vision, the ability to motivate their teams effectively, and the capacity to make quick and sound decisions.

I would like to share my own experiences regarding how different leadership styles can impact organisational performance.

My first advice is to always be adaptable to change, resilient, and committed when leading your organisation.

Executive leadership is more than just being a business leader.

Executive leadership entails more than simply guiding an organisation toward its goals; it also involves creating an environment where everyone feels valued, understands their roles and expectations, and feels empowered to achieve the objectives set by the leadership team.

Executive leaders are responsible for defining and pursuing the organisation's mission. They play a key role in creating and setting strategic goals, ensuring that all parts of the organisation align with these objectives. This role requires individuals who have drive, passion, and a diverse set of skills.

Successful executive leaders think and act swiftly and decisively. They possess strong interpersonal skills and recognize the importance of each team member's contribution to the organisation.

EXECUTIVE LEADERSHIP PRINCIPLES

① Strategic Direction and Vision

A compelling vision is essential for the success of any organisation. It serves as a guide for decision-making and inspires employees to align their efforts with the organisation's goals. Leaders should engage in strategic planning to create a clear vision that encompasses both short-term objectives and long-term aspirations. This vision must be communicated effectively at all levels of the organisation, using storytelling techniques that resonate emotionally with employees, thereby encouraging a sense of belonging and purpose among the workforce.

② Communication

Effective communication is crucial for successful leadership. Leaders need to clearly convey their vision, expectations, and strategies. It is also important for them to create a culture of open communication, where team members feel comfortable sharing their ideas and feedback. This two-way communication builds trust and encourages collaboration and problem-solving. To maintain transparency and engagement, regular updates, town hall meetings, and informal check-ins can be beneficial.

③ Ethical Leadership and Integrity

Integrity is the cornerstone of effective leadership. Leaders who exhibit ethical behaviour inspire trust and commitment within their teams. By making ethical decisions and holding themselves accountable, these leaders cultivate a culture of integrity that impacts the entire organisation. This commitment to ethical leadership makes employees feel safe and valued, which in turn enhances their job satisfaction and loyalty. Ultimately, by prioritizing ethical decision-making and accountability, leaders foster an environment where integrity thrives throughout the organisation.

④ Resilience and Adaptability

Change and adaptability are essential qualities for leaders. They must be willing to adjust their strategies in response to new information, shifting market dynamics, and technological advancements. Resilience—the ability to bounce back from setbacks—is equally important. Leaders should foster a growth mindset, encouraging their teams to see challenges as opportunities for learning and improvement rather than as obstacles.

⑤ Empowering and Delegation

Effective leaders empower their teams by delegating authority and encouraging autonomy. This empowerment creates a sense of ownership and accountability among team members, resulting in higher levels of engagement and innovation. By trusting team members to lead projects and make decisions, leaders can foster a collaborative environment where diverse ideas are welcomed and explored.

EXECUTIVE LEADERSHIP CHALLENGES

Executive leadership is rewarding but presents numerous challenges that can hinder the achievement of organisational goals. Understanding these challenges is essential for effective leadership.

① Navigating Change

Organisations often encounter significant changes due to factors such as technological advancements, market fluctuations, and regulatory updates. Leaders must manage these transitions effectively by providing guidance and support to ensure their teams stay focused and motivated. Implementing change management strategies, such as clear communication plans and training sessions, can help employees adapt to new processes and systems.

② Diverse Teams Management

A diverse workforce brings a variety of perspectives but also poses challenges in communication and collaboration. Leaders must cultivate an inclusive environment that values diversity and promotes equity. This requires understanding different cultural backgrounds and establishing policies that support inclusion. Leaders should also implement training programs focused on diversity, equity, and inclusion (DEI) to equip employees with the skills needed to navigate these dynamics effectively.

③ Short-term and Long-term Goals

Executives often feel pressured to achieve short-term results while also planning for long-term sustainability. Balancing these competing priorities is crucial for the health of the organisation. Leaders need to establish clear priorities and allocate resources effectively, ensuring that immediate actions align with the overall strategic vision. It is essential for leaders to model balanced behavior, encouraging their teams to take breaks and manage their workloads effectively to maintain overall well-being.

STRATEGIES FOR EFFECTIVE EXECUTIVE LEADERSHIP

To effectively address challenges and enhance their leadership, executives can adopt several strategies:

① Fostering Decision-Making challenges

Executives frequently encounter complex decisions with limited information. It is crucial for them to analyze risks, consult with stakeholders, and make informed choices. Leaders should be comfortable navigating ambiguity and making timely decisions, relying on both quantitative data and qualitative insights from their teams.

② Work-Life Balance

The demands of executive leadership can lead to burnout for both leaders and their teams. Prioritising self-care and promoting a healthy work-life balance within the organisation fosters a collaborative work culture.

③ Collaboration

Collaboration fosters creativity and innovation. Leaders should cultivate an environment that promotes teamwork, idea-sharing, and cross-functional projects. This can be accomplished through team-building activities, collaborative technology tools, and a culture that values collective achievements.

④ Professional Development Investment

Continuous learning is vital for both leaders and their teams. Offering professional development opportunities such as training sessions, workshops, and mentorship programs helps employees enhance their skills and prepares them for future challenges. Leaders should also prioritize their own growth through executive coaching and leadership training.

⑤ Technology

Technology enhances communication and streamlines operations effectively. Leaders should adopt digital tools that promote collaboration, data analysis, and project management. By utilizing technology, organisations can boost efficiency and make informed decisions based on real-time data.

⑥ Set Clear Goals and Key performance indicators (Metrics)

Setting clear objectives and performance metrics enables leaders to monitor progress and make informed decisions based on data. This transparency aligns team efforts and promotes accountability. Regular reviews and adjustments to goals ensure that the organisation stays focused on its strategic priorities.

⑦ Innovation

Creating a culture that embraces experimentation and innovation can lead to significant breakthroughs. Leaders should encourage teams to take calculated risks and explore new ideas without fear of failure. By celebrating successes and learning from failures, organisations reinforce a culture of continuous improvement.

THE IMPACT OF LEADERSHIP STYLES ON ORGANISATIONAL PERFORMANCE

Different leadership styles can profoundly influence organisational performance. Here are several common styles and their implications:

① Leadership - Transformational

Transformational leaders inspire their teams to exceed expectations by fostering a culture of innovation and personal development. They encourage creativity and empower employees to take ownership of their work. This leadership style often results in high levels of engagement and commitment, ultimately driving organisational success.

② Leadership - Transactional

This leadership style emphasizes structure, rewards, and performance metrics. While it may lead to short-term success, it often does not promote the long-term engagement needed for sustainable growth. Transactional leaders typically depend on clear directives and performance-based rewards, which can stifle creativity and initiative.

③ Leadership - Servant

Servant leaders prioritise the needs of their team members and encourage a supportive environment that enhances employee satisfaction and retention. By focusing on the growth and well-being of their teams, servant leaders cultivate a committed and productive workforce.

④ Leadership - Situational

Situational leaders adjust their leadership style according to the specific context and needs of their team. This adaptability enables them to effectively tackle various challenges and fosters a dynamic organisational culture that can succeed in changing environments.

⑤ Leadership - Authentic

Authentic leaders build trust through transparency and honesty. By staying true to their values and principles, they build strong relationships and cultivate a positive organisational culture. This trust can result in increased employee engagement and loyalty, thereby enhancing overall performance.

In Summary

Executive leadership requires a clear vision, strong communication skills, integrity, and adaptability.

Organisations are facing increasing complexities and challenges, both internally and externally. Therefore, the ability to lead effectively has become critical.

Executive leaders play a crucial role in guiding an organisation through challenges and towards achieving its goals. By understanding the principles of effective leadership and addressing operational difficulties, they can implement successful strategies that steer the organisation in the right direction.

Effective executive leadership improves and enhances an organisation's overall performance.

Establishing strong benchmarks and having a clear, concise business vision, along with well-defined goals, is essential for guiding all team members. Effective executive leadership recognises the continual need to grow, adapt, and embrace change.

Leaders must remain committed to developing and enhancing their skills, embracing diversity, and fostering a culture of inclusion, collaboration and future innovation.

By doing so, executive leaders will ensure that their organisations are not left behind and can position themselves effectively for both the present and the future while also meeting the needs and requirements necessary for the organization to flourish and succeed.

Here are the top qualities that make an excellent leader:

- Lead by example
- Cultivate a growth mindset
- Commit to continuous learning
- Instill a sense of purpose
- Celebrate achievements
- Create a safe learning environment

- Inspire with passion
- Develop emotional intelligence
- Prioritise physical and mental well-being
- Encourage reflection

ABOUT DR. JEAN KFOURY

AUSTRALIA

Bio/CV:

- Professional Athlete in the sport of Taekwondo, 9th dan grandmaster
- Current elected Australian Taekwondo national president
- Current 2024 elected vice president (Oceania) for the Commonwealth Taekwondo Union
- 2013 Official Induction Taekwondo Hall of Fame: outstanding Taekwondo player

Academic Qualification:

- Grandmaster
- 9th dan Chun Do Kwan
- 8th dan Kukkiwon
- Doctor of Philosphy

CHAPTER FOURTEEN

THE INFLUENCE OF CONFIDENCE, DISCIPLINE & RESPECT IN LEADERSHIP

BY STEPHEN MILLER

My father was a man of few words, but when he spoke, those words were usually powerful, and people listened. I was always amazed by the way everyone responded to him and how he commanded the room he was in. Whether he was coaching football or baseball for the local community, players were naturally drawn to him, and the parents appreciated his coaching style. I was always in awe of my father. When I was young, I was quite reserved. Although I had some friends, I spent more time at home than outside playing like most kids. As a high school student, I faced many challenges and struggled to fit in. While I got along with everyone, I never felt I had a close circle of friends. I often felt disconnected from my peers and had difficulty finding my place at school. It seemed like everyone else had their cliques and friendships figured out, leaving me feeling like an outsider. I never commanded a room or a group of people like my father did. As a result, my self-esteem and confidence suffered, leading to minor depression. I also faced challenges in sports, where I struggled to keep up and felt inadequate. Despite this, I loved playing baseball in the city league, especially with my father as my coach.

However, in high school, feeling isolated and lacking confidence, I chose not to participate in the one activity I truly enjoyed. My parents saw this and kept encouraging me, and as a result, I tried wrestling. Having never done it before, I quickly became familiar with the lights by name because most of the surrounding schools had feeder programs for the sport. Unfortunately, my final record as a freshman wrestler was 0-16, which contributed to my feelings of frustration and low self-esteem. Despite this, I genuinely enjoyed wrestling, so I began working out independently, joined a gym, and signed up for summer clinics. While this effort helped somewhat, I finished my sophomore season with a record of 3–12. I realized I was still missing something and seriously considered not returning for my junior year.

As I struggled to find success, I took a deep look at myself and realized that a significant part of the problem was my tendency to be a follower rather than a leader like my father. I never seemed to command a room. But why was that? What was missing that prevented me from becoming stronger and more leadership-oriented?

At this point, I took my first martial arts class at American Tae Kwon Do, taught by Grandmaster Dae Kyu Lee. Here, I realized the essential components of leadership: confidence, discipline, and respect. This experience initiated my growth in three crucial areas that helped transform me into a stronger leader. As a result, I advanced in the dental field from an accounts receivable position to my current role as Director of Operations for a major DSO. Additionally, I opened my own Taekwondo school in Absecon, New Jersey.

Confidence

Training in martial arts has profoundly impacted my confidence. I have built self-assurance, mental resilience, and self-esteem through physical activity, mental focus, and repetitive routines. As I progressed in my training, I experienced a transformation that extended beyond physical skills and began influencing my daily life and interactions with others.

One significant way martial arts increased my confidence was by allowing me to set realistic, attainable goals and celebrate my achievements through belt promotions. I still remember the first time I attempted to break a board. I missed it, and it didn't break. However, I was encouraged to try again and again until it finally broke. This accomplishment, along with many others throughout my training, reinforced my sense of pride and capability, ultimately fostering greater confidence in my abilities.

Martial arts taught me the values of perseverance and resilience. Through training, I learned to face and overcome challenges, developing skills to handle difficult situations better. Competing in tournaments forced me to confront my inadequacy fears and push beyond my comfort zone. This experience helped me become mentally tougher and gain confidence in my ability to manage distress.

A key lesson I learned in martial arts, which is crucial for building confidence and essential for leadership, is the importance of having a supportive team and positive role models around you. Instructors, as leaders, play a vital role in encouraging and motivating each other, fostering a sense of belonging and shared purpose. This type of environment enables students or employees to develop a strong, positive self-image and helps them feel a sense of purpose in their school or workplace.

Training in martial arts has significantly enhanced my mindfulness and self-awareness. I have gained a deeper understanding of my thoughts, emotions, and behaviors, leading me to realize the profound impact of martial arts on my confidence. I have developed a strong sense of self-belief and assurance through setting and achieving goals, building resilience, and receiving support from instructors and fellow students in the community. This newfound confidence empowers me to face life's challenges with balance and determination.

Leading with confidence and learning to instill all these traits in your team members is key to being successful.

Discipline

For those who have studied or learned about martial arts, the concept of discipline is a fundamental aspect. It typically serves as the core foundation of the practice. Through rigorous training, adherence to tradition, and a commitment to continuous self-improvement, martial arts training cultivates a strong sense of discipline. This discipline extends beyond the physical techniques learned, influencing the development of both the mind and emotions. When training in a martial art, discipline is fostered in several ways:

- **Repeated actions** – I have learned that when we practice techniques and drills thousands of times, we develop a high level of muscle memory. This allows our bodies to react to situations without overthinking. As a result, we can respond effectively, regardless of our stress level.
- **Feedback/Correction** – Effective instructors regularly provide feedback to help us improve as martial artists. Feedback should be both affirming and corrective, but it must never be harsh.

- **Detail-Oriented** – Focusing on the correct actions and movements helps create a higher level of detail and accuracy. When I teach a class, I emphasize to my students the importance of training with 100% effort and never taking it easy. How you practice is how you will perform when it truly matters. This principle applies in the dojang and all aspects of life—always strive to give your best effort. If your team sees that you are not fully committed, they may question why they should be.
- **Respect for tradition** – In martial arts, the importance of tradition is widely recognized, as most disciplines are passed down through generations. To preserve the integrity of the art, we must respect the instructors who taught us and strive to impart that same level of skill and knowledge to our students. Similarly, as leaders, it is essential to align ourselves with the philosophy of the organization we work for and adhere to the standards the company aims to uphold.
- **Self-control** – Regardless of whether you are in martial arts or any other situation, it is essential to learn how to manage your emotions and thoughts. Being self-aware is crucial. As a leader, your team needs to observe that you maintain a consistent emotional state, no matter the circumstances. This demonstrates to them that you are in control at all times, which in turn helps to sustain their confidence in you.
- **Focus and Priorities** - A strong focus allows you to avoid distractions.
- **Adaptability** - Regardless of the situation you face, a good leader must be able to adapt, change direction, and be innovative at all times to ensure the team's success.

- **Discipline and Integrity** - A leader who acts with discipline demonstrates integrity by always doing the right thing, whether or not someone is watching.

By implementing these strategies, you will achieve higher levels of accountability, maintain focus on tasks, and enhance your ability to adapt when necessary. A good leader takes responsibility not only for their own actions but also for the actions and decisions of the team.

Respect

Respect has always been important to me to some degree. My father was one of the most respectful people I know, and from him, I learned the fundamentals of respect. I learned never to interrupt someone while speaking, not to play with or break other people's belongings, and to always address my elders as "sir" or "ma'am." However, I never fully realized how significant respect would become in society.

After I began training in martial arts, I quickly discovered that respect is one of its core values. This includes respect for oneself, fellow students, instructors, the dojang, the equipment, and the art itself. I trained there every day, often participating in two classes. The training was challenging, but Grandmaster Lee and the other instructors served as excellent mentors. They taught me not just the sport itself but also the tradition and history behind it. This experience has profoundly influenced how I lead my students at my dojang and manage my employees at the office.

Through my training, respect was encouraged in various ways:

- **Tradition and authority** – Actions such as bowing before entering or leaving the training floor, bowing to higher belts and addressing them by their correct titles, and lining up by rank help to foster respect.

- **Guidance** – All instructors show and teach respect by providing guidance and giving feedback to facilitate student progression.
- **Etiquette** – In all my training, every class is highly structured, and the instructors emphasize the importance of using correct techniques. My students understand that if I notice their block is off by even a quarter of an inch, I will come over and adjust their hand to the proper position. This continuous correction of mistakes helps to foster respect for the traditions of the arts.
- **Working together** – By collaborating, we can support each other during challenging sessions and offer positive advice.

The respect you demonstrate will extend beyond your current role and positively influence your leadership skills in various ways. You will learn to approach your team with empathy and understanding, enhancing communication. Taking the time to understand each other fosters clearer conversations.

As mentioned earlier, accountability and integrity are also shaped by respect, as it encourages you to uphold high standards not only for your team but for yourself as well. Additionally, respect fosters humility; by valuing your employees' opinions and suggestions and by taking responsibility for your own mistakes, you create a more collaborative environment. Over the years, many parents have approached me, sharing how their child's behavior at home or academic performance has improved since they began their training.

By mastering the three key areas of confidence, discipline, and respect, you can become a much better leader than you might believe.

ABOUT STEPHEN MILLER

USA

Grandmaster Stephen Miller was born and raised in Northfield, NJ, and currently lives in Egg Harbor Township, NJ, with his wife, Robin, and their two dogs. On his 16th birthday, his parents gifted him his first lessons at the local Taekwondo school. Forty-one years later, he continues to train and teach.

Accomplishments:

- Holds a seventh-degree black belt from the United States National Taekwondo Federation.
- Holds a fifth-degree black belt from the Kukkiwon, in South Korea, and had the honor of testing there in 2019.
- Holds a first-degree black belt in the art of Koyro Gumdo (Korean swords), from the World Koryo Gumdo Association. He is the only black belt in this art in the state of New Jersey.
- 2012 International Champion in Poomse

- 2023: Inducted into the Masters of Martial Arts Hall of Fame and won the Gold Medal as the Best Martial Arts Studio in the Best Of The Press contest
- 2024: Inducted into both the Action Martial Arts Magazine and the American Martial Arts Alliance Hall of Honor
- Trained in South Korea on three occasions: 1988, 2008, and 2019 to further his knowledge.

FOR MORE INFORMATION:

- CDR Taekwondo
- Website: www.cdr-tkd.com
- Email: stmiller22@hotmail.com

CHAPTER FIFTEEN

LEADERSHIP BY EXAMPLE

BY MICHAEL SULLENGER

During my years as a military officer, commander, police chief, college professor, and martial arts instructor, I have always tried to address more than just the physical aspects of leading and teaching others. One must understand that leadership also involves managing and mentoring those you lead. While the definitions differ, they go hand-in-glove when you are in a leadership role. Understanding your people's needs, capabilities, and desires is crucial to knowing how to guide them. The demands of leadership also depend on the size of the organization or, as a martial arts instructor, the number of students you teach. I mentioned the size of the organization because the bigger it is, the less time you have to get to know and work with those you lead and the more you must delegate.

What follows are some examples of experiences I've had during my career in different leadership positions. This will start when I returned to the Air Force in 1977; I had been enlisted for four years, followed by my last tour of duty before retiring in 1993. Once back in civilian life, we'll look at my experiences as a college professor. Last, we will look at my final years as a police chief. I will cover my approaches to and lessons learned as a leader in each of these areas.

A key to being a good leader is using the talent that exists within the organization. Whether I was commanding a security police squadron or running a police department in civilian life, I always took advantage of the knowledge and experience of those I lead. The decision was ultimately mine to make. I did not have to make those decisions in a vacuum. By bringing others into the decision-making process, you also give them ownership of the organization. The feeling they get from being a part of this process makes for a more cohesive leadership team where people feel a sense of value.

I also follow the "leadership by example" model. As a leader, you should be able and willing to do what you ask others to do. When I returned to the Air Force as a newly minted 2nd lieutenant in 1977, stationed at Tinker AFB, I was made the department's SWAT commander. One afternoon, I went to see what the training sergeant had the guys doing, only to find them practicing repelling at the four-story fire tower. The training sergeant said, "Hey, LT, you need to come up here and try this." What the sergeant did not know was I have a real fear of heights. Following the leadership by example belief, I climbed up to the top, put on the Swiss seat, and got ready to repel. If the reader understands the term "minus five pucker factor," you will know how scared I was.

By the time I got to the ground on that first repel, I realized it wasn't that bad. I went back up three more times. Great training. Also, the best way I know of to improve one's self-confidence is by getting out of your comfort zone and letting those you lead see you right there with them.

At the end of my military career, I was stationed at Chanute Air Force Base in Rantoul, Illinois. I was the commander and chief of the security police of the base. While walking through my building, I came across two young airmen unloading a truck. They were placing boxes of printing paper on a cart to deliver to the various offices in our building. I stopped and greeted them. After a short conversation, I helped them unload the truck. They both looked at me in shock. "Sir," one of the young men said, "you're not supposed to be doing that!" I asked him, "Why?" He said, "Well, sir, you're the commander." I said, "Nothing in my job description says I'm not supposed to do this type of work." I went on to tell them while I was the commander, I was also part of the team. That being the case, I was helping my teammates finish their tasks a little quicker. I also explained that my rank merely meant I had more responsibilities than they did, but that didn't preclude me from giving them a hand. A good leader should never have the attitude a job or task is beneath him if his people are involved in doing it.

During my teaching years at two different community colleges, I taught Saturday morning classes for five years. After one class, a female student in her forties approached me. She told me she really enjoyed my class and had taken it because her daughter had been one of my students three years earlier. I asked her where her daughter was. She told me she had finished her sophomore year at a four-year university. I said that was great and asked her what her daughter had decided to major in. She told me she majored in political science because she wanted to teach government classes like mine. I can't begin to tell you the great feeling of satisfaction and accomplishment that gave me.

On Friday, August 31, 2007, I was reunited with a former martial arts student I had not seen in some thirty years. When we last saw each other (circa 1976), David Aguilar had been selected to enter the United States Border Patrol. He was anxious about leaving home, as most young people are. It's not easy to leave the comfort and security of what you know to enter places and situations you don't. I told David he had a wonderful opportunity in front of him. I explained that a door had opened that would allow him to do whatever he would set his sights on. Little did I know he would one day become the chief of the whole U.S. Border Patrol.

David and I were able to reconnect via email a few years later. He shared with me the influence I had on him, both from the standpoint of the four years of karate training and the fatherly advice about being a responsible citizen and making the best of the opportunities that would present themselves. I was interested in the possibility of him coming to the college campus where I was teaching as an associate professor to share this with my students, as well as anyone else who would care to listen. After working with his aide, Tim Sullivan, arrangements were made, and the wheels were set in motion. Tim asked me what I wanted the chief to talk about. I told him he could talk about the missions the border patrol has, but what I was really interested in him talking about was how anyone can achieve the American dream if they apply themselves.

Chief Aguilar spoke that Friday before a group of 200 students and faculty at Texas State Technical College in Harlingen, Texas, where I am in my eleventh year of teaching American and Texas Government. He told the audience of his years growing up in South Texas along the border when he would pick fruit or produce on weekends to make some extra money. The experiences he shared with the students were those many could relate to. His example to them of the American Dream in persona and role model could not have been better.

In my last department as the police chief, after retiring from teaching, I met with my personnel for the first time. I told them one of my responsibilities was to replace myself. One of the officers asked me what I meant. I told them that one example was training another range master who could ensure all the officers were qualified. I was the only one with those qualifications at the time. I also asked if any of them would like to sit in the chief's chair one day to let me know so we could look at what training and education I could help them get, which would set the stage for that possibility down the road. Sadly, no one took me up on the offer. One of the things a leader learns about those under them is not everyone has the motivation to move up. Far too many are satisfied with the status quo and don't want any added responsibilities.

As you work with people, you develop an idea of each one's capabilities as a learner, along with areas where they struggle. You try to manage classes (whether academic or martial arts) in a way that allows for those who advance quickly to do so while still paying close attention to those who are slower in physical abilities or their mental grasp of a given concept.

The development of good skills and mechanics in kicking and punching are combined with a proper attitude and outlook toward the future. A leader must also be aware of how they are perceived by those they lead. Students look up to their sensei for guidance in more than just technique. Likewise, many of the college students I taught were changed by me challenging them to make good decisions by applying critical thinking skills.

What does this tell us about being leaders? It illustrates our tremendous responsibility to help our students focus on their physical and mental abilities to prepare them for life as adults in our society. We must instill in them the importance of being the best they can be, whether competing in the ring or being a functioning member of society in everyday life. Sadly, most of us never learn whether we have had a positive impact on our students. I can tell you the satisfaction I have gotten from learning the part I played in David's life is beyond words. I can also say how blessed I feel to have been able to learn about his feelings regarding our early relationship and the positive effect it had on his life and his later success.

Over the years, I have been blessed to learn from different comments and observations made by those I've influenced in one way or another that I have been a positive one. Regardless of the duration of our relationship or contact, the result was one where they took away an improved outlook on life, as well as an improved set of skills. As a Christian, I genuinely believe God gives each of us the opportunity to influence others at some time or place in our lives. Realizing this is a key to understanding the awesome responsibility that is.

When I first put on a black belt in May of 1968, I never realized the importance my actions would have as an instructor. I did not realize I would be able to influence the lives of others by my leadership. As I have gotten older, I've come to realize the importance of my actions, as well as the responsibility I had taken upon myself as I taught others who looked up to me as a role model and mentor. This realization grew as my leadership roles and responsibilities did over the years. First as an officer in the U.S. Air Force Security Forces and later as an associate professor, assistant police chief, and chief.

Each of you must be aware of this every time you step on the floor of the dojo to teach others. Take responsibility seriously. Follow the guidance about leading by example and ensure the example you are setting is a proper one. If you do, you may well have the opportunity one day to experience the wonderful feeling of satisfaction in knowing the positive impact you had on someone else's life.

ABOUT MICHAEL SULLENGER

USA

Michael A. Sullenger, Major, USAF-SF, retired; Associate Professor (Criminal Justice & Political Science) retired; Police Chief (49+ years) retired. Author of Memoirs & Political Observations - A View from Flyover Country; Co-author of American & Texas Government, Horizon Publication (text & workbook); and has published numerous articles on martial arts and police training found on Martialforce.com, USAdojo.com, and Official Karate Magazine.

He is a use of force & combative instructor for Texas Law Enforcement.

Mike's years of study and training have taken him from Indiana, his birth state, to Texas, Oklahoma, Illinois, Alabama, Mexico, Spain, England, and Germany. He either found places to train or started classes. This resulted in his fluency in Spanish and German, where he taught the economies of both countries.

Mike is a founding member of the American Karate System, joining with Ernest Lieb and the heads of 12 other schools from several different states in 1973.

His achievements include:

- 9th Dan Chief Instructor - Emeritus, American Karate System
- 10th Dan Tanaka AikiJujut su-Budo/Soryu Karate Daito ryu
- 10th Dan South Texas Karate Black Belt Association
- 2008 Master's Hall of Fame Inductee
- 2023 United States Martial Arts Hall of Fame Inductee
- 2024 Universal Martial Arts Hall of Fame Inductee

FOR MORE INFORMATION:

- Website: www.aks-usa.com
- Email: kick2aks@yahoo.com

SECRETS TO

BUSINESS

CHAPTER SIXTEEN

THE SECRETS TO BUSINESS SUCCESS FROM A MARTIAL ARTS PERSPECTIVE

BY DENNIS BROWN

In both martial arts and business, the fundamental principles remain the same: discipline, vision, focus, and perseverance. Throughout my years as a martial artist, coach, and business entrepreneur, I've learned that success doesn't come from quick wins or shortcuts—it comes from an unwavering commitment to growth, learning, and innovation. In this chapter, I will share with you the secrets I've learned along the way to turning martial arts principles into business success.

The Early Years: From Passion to Profession

Life has a way of guiding us toward our purpose in ways we might not fully understand at first. For me, that guidance came through martial arts. It all began at a young age when I found myself searching for something more—something that would not only challenge me physically but also mentally and spiritually. Little did I know that my journey into martial arts would evolve into a lifelong passion, and eventually, a mission to inspire others through the opening of my own professional martial arts school.

When I first embarked on my martial arts journey, I envisioned a career centered purely on teaching—on passing down the techniques and principles that had transformed my own life. I assumed that if I opened my school, students would naturally walk through the door, eager to learn. Little did I know, the path to running a successful martial arts school was far more complex, and the idea of simply "teaching" was only the tip of the iceberg.

In the early days, many martial arts schools, including my own, opened in less-than-ideal locations, often in areas where access to resources and opportunities was limited. Despite our passion for the art, too many schools opened and closed, unable to stay afloat. The financial side of the business was often overlooked, and we struggled with attracting and retaining students. It wasn't until the mid-60s that things began to change. This shift was due in large part to three innovators in the martial arts business world: Grandmaster Jhoon Rhee, Nicholas Cokinos and of course, my Kung-Fu Master Teacher, Grandmaster Willy Lin, to whom I owe my long and inspiring career.

The Turning Point: Learning from the Innovators

Nicholas Cokinos was a visionary who understood that the key to sustaining a martial arts school was not only teaching excellence but also building a strong, sustainable business model. Through his teachings, I began to understand that a martial arts school should be run like any other professional business, with systems, structure, and a clear focus on customer service and community engagement. He instilled in me the importance of treating martial arts as a profession, not just a passion.

Mr. Cokinos, owner and manager of seven Art Linkletter Dance Studios and an expert in business management came to my school one day and invited me to join the EFC (Educational Funding Company) Board that was dedicated to the growth of martial arts schools, where I would be introduced to a whole new world of business principles.

Mr. Cokinos took the time to teach me about the business strategies that had made the Art Linkletter Dance Studios so successful—principles like the importance of branding, marketing, creating a positive customer experience, and developing efficient operational systems. These lessons were eye-opening. I began to understand that, just as in martial arts, the key to success in business was not only about mastering techniques but also about developing a clear and effective strategy. I learned that martial arts schools needed to run like any other business—focused on profitability, scalability, and growth.

The Realization: Martial Arts and Business Are Two Sides of the Same Coin

The lessons I learned from Grandmaster Jhoon Rhee, Nicholas Cokinos and Grandmaster Willy Lin marked a critical turning point in my martial arts career. It was no longer just about training students—it was about creating a business model that could sustain and grow a school for the long term. I began to treat my school as a professional business, adopting systems for everything from student retention to marketing, sales, and financial management.

The first major realization was that success in martial arts, just like in business, was about more than just passion—it was about strategy, planning, and execution. The second realization was that martial arts schools needed to be located in areas that were accessible to the community, and they needed to offer a level of service that kept students coming back, year after year.

As my school began to grow, I applied the business principles I had learned, including developing a strong branding strategy and focusing on customer relationships. I started investing in marketing, improving the student experience, and offering additional programs to retain students long-term. For example, we began to offer more specialized classes, like self-defense and leadership programs, that appealed to a broader audience. I also learned the importance of hiring and training qualified staff, building a professional atmosphere, and creating a curriculum that offered consistent value to students.

Fifty Years Later: The Continued Evolution of My Martial Arts School

Looking back over the past fifty years, I can say with certainty that those early lessons I learned about the business side of martial arts transformed my life and the life of my school. The combination of passion for the art and a solid business foundation became the cornerstone of my success.

Today, my martial arts school is not just a place where students come to learn; it is a thriving, professional institution that serves as a model for how martial arts schools can succeed in the modern world. The lessons I learned from Grandmaster Jhoon Rhee, Nicholas Cokinos and Grandmaster Willy Lin continue to guide me, and I am constantly seeking new ways to improve and evolve the business side of my school.

I now understand that being a martial arts instructor is about much more than teaching technique; it's about creating an environment where students can grow, feel supported, and achieve their personal goals. It's about running a professional business that adds value to the community, supports its staff, and helps the art of martial arts continue to thrive for generations to come.

The Legacy: Teaching the Next Generation of Martial Artists and Entrepreneurs

As I continue to teach and run my school, my focus is not only on training the next generation of martial artists but also on preparing them to be successful business owners, teachers, and leaders. I now incorporate the business principles I've learned into my teachings, ensuring that my students understand that martial arts is not just about physical prowess—it's about leadership, responsibility, and professionalism.

Opening a martial arts school is no longer a matter of simply teaching the art; it is about creating a lasting institution that can serve the community for decades. As I reflect on my own journey, I see how martial arts and business are two sides of the same coin, each feeding into the other, creating a balanced and fulfilling career.

The lessons I've learned over the past fifty plus years continue to shape my approach to martial arts and life. And while I'm proud of the school I've built, I am even prouder of the students whose lives I've touched along the way. They are the true legacy of my journey, and I will continue to serve them and the martial arts community for as long as I can.

The Impact: How Martial Arts Changed My Life

Opening my martial arts school was the beginning of a new chapter in my life. It was a journey that brought challenges and triumphs, but it was also the fulfillment of a long-held passion. Over the years, I've seen countless students walk through the doors of my school, many of them facing their own personal struggles, and I've had the privilege of watching them transform.

Through the years, I've witnessed students grow not only in their martial arts abilities but also in their personal lives. Some came to me seeking physical strength, while others came looking for mental clarity, self-confidence, or a sense of belonging. As they progressed, I saw them develop a greater sense of purpose, a deeper respect for themselves and others, and a newfound resilience that helped them face challenges both inside and outside the school. These transformations have been the most rewarding part of my journey.

Running a martial arts school has also had a profound impact on my own life. It's deepened my understanding of leadership, patience, and empathy. I've had to learn how to balance the responsibilities of being a teacher, a mentor, and a business owner. Every day, I strive to be a better role model for my students, to lead with integrity, and to help them reach their full potential. The lessons I've taught and the students I've mentored have in turn taught me invaluable lessons about perseverance, humility, and the importance of lifelong learning.

The school has also become a place of community, where friendships are formed, and a sense of camaraderie is built. It's humbling to see how martial arts has brought people together, how it's helped them connect with others in meaningful ways, and how it's become a family of like-minded individuals who support one another both in the school and in life.

ABOUT DENNIS BROWN

USA

Grand Master Dennis Brown, an accomplished businessman, martial arts event promoter, on-screen actor, and competitor, was rated #1 in the country during his competition years.

Highly regarded in the martial arts business community:

- President and Founder – Dennis Brown Shaolin WuShu Center
- Lifelong U.S.A. Chairman – Wang-Qihe Taijiquan Association, Heibei, China
- Founding Board Member – Educational Funding Company
- Board Member – North American Sport Karate Association
- Business Hall of Fame – Educational Management Company

One of the most influential martial artists in the country:

- First African American to study martial arts in China, 1982.
- Certifications from Jiangsu Sports Center in Nanjing and Beijing Institute of Physical Education.
- Black Belt Hall of Fame and Inside Kung Fu Hall of Fame. Cited as one of the "25 Most Influential Martial Artists of the 20th Century."
- Founder and promoter of the 6-A rated US Capitol Classics China Open international martial arts event
- Only American to represent China's leading style of Tai Chi and meditation in the U.S.
- Featured in the Smithsonian American Art Museum exhibition: Sightlines: Chinatown & Beyond
- Lead Actor, "The Warrior," motion picture
- Featured in: "Secrets of the Warriors Powers," a Discovery Channel Documentary; "The Black Kung-Fu Experience," a PBS Documentary; "How I Made It In America," a national documentary
- Hosted "Martial Arts Showcase," Talk Show

FOR MORE INFORMATION:

- Dennis Brown Shaolin Wu-Shu Center
- Website: www.dennisbrownshaolin.com
- Email: dennisbrownkungfu@gmail.com
- Facebook: @dennis.brown.77377692

CHAPTER SEVENTEEN

BUSINESS ASPECTS OF TAEKWONDO

BY JOHN CONNELLY

Introduction

Taekwondo is renowned for its powerful kicking techniques. Over the last 50 years, the practice of Taekwondo has grown globally, continually increasing in popularity.

Let's explore how the teachings and practices of Taekwondo benefit practitioners in their personal, professional, and business lives. From this point on, I will refer to martial arts practitioners as students as we continue to examine the business aspects and teachings of Taekwondo.

Historical Beginnings:

Taekwondo has its origins in Korea and has evolved from ancient martial arts Taekkyeon and Subak. Modern martial arts, including Tang Soo Do and Hapkido, have also influenced various aspects of Taekwondo. Over time, Taekwondo has adapted and changed before formalizing into its current art form. This process of change is a natural evolution and has become fundamental in the workplace and business world.

The Korea Taekwondo Association was established in 1955, followed by the creation of the World Taekwondo Federation in 1973. These organizations were formed to standardize Taekwondo practices while promoting its teachings worldwide in a controlled manner. This has also enabled the art to maintain unified standards and practices.

Philosophy and Principles taught:

The main principle of Taekwondo is "Do," which translates to "the way" or "the path."

Taekwondo serves not only as a means of physical improvement and combat skills but also as a method for enhancing one's life through guiding tenets.

These tenets emphasize the importance of courtesy, integrity, perseverance, and self-control, fostering the development of an indomitable spirit. Instructors use these principles to guide their students' training and interactions both inside and outside the dojang (training hall).

Respect is taught to everyone involved. The lessons on integrity and perseverance help students confront personal challenges, while the emphasis on self-control equips them to handle conflicts effectively.

Personal Development:

Following the principles taught enhances the following aspects:

- Personal confidence
- Mental resilience
- Emotional maturity
- Spiritual growth
- Discipline

Training also teaches how to set goals, plan effectively, prepare thoroughly, and achieve desired outcomes. It instills the ability to overcome any obstacles that may arise while working towards these goals. Additionally, training offers benefits such as increased self-confidence and self-esteem, as individuals develop their skills and gain confidence in their abilities.

Students learn to use both mental and physical tools to overcome new challenges. The confidence gained from training provides students with a deeper understanding of their abilities and limitations. By cultivating self-assurance and humility, they discover how to reach their full potential.

Leadership:

Instructors not only teach martial arts skills but also foster the development of strong leadership abilities. Training provides students the chance to stand before the class and lead sessions, helping them enhance their vocal skills and learn to speak confidently while giving clear, concise, and specific instructions. They also learn to understand how different students respond and are motivated in class.

By utilizing auditory, visual, and kinesthetic teaching methods, students engage in open communication, learning to listen and effectively express themselves. Instructors emphasize the importance of empathy, which significantly contributes to building successful business relationships.

Students are taught to communicate assertively. The leadership skills developed through this training are directly applicable in the business world, where effective leaders aim to inspire, motivate, and guide others toward shared visions and goals.

Teamwork:

Training creates teamwork.

Example: Students participate in group training, sparring sessions, and team competitions, which require them to work effectively together. During these sessions, they learn to communicate, cooperate, and support one another.

Effective teamwork is crucial in the business world, where success often depends on individuals' ability to collaborate toward common goals and objectives. Students who grasp the skills and benefits of teamwork are better equipped to work alongside colleagues.

They learn to assign tasks, leverage the strengths of their team members, and create a positive and supportive workplace environment.

Conflict Resolution:

Students are taught to resolve conflicts in a peaceful and respectful manner. Conflicts can occur at any time.

Example: Personality Differences Leading to Poor Attitude and Behavior in Class:

In a class, we observe different personalities, particularly between Student A and Student B. Student B wishes to concentrate on their training and wants to make the most out of every session, while Student A tends to act out and joke around.

To address these differences in a constructive and positive manner, we require problem-management skills from our students. Effective and respectful communication is essential.

In this scenario, Student A is having a difficult day, and eventually, Student B comes to realize this. Both students decide to step out of the class and agree to discuss the issue respectfully. This decision allows the class to continue without disruption, enabling other students to get back to their training.

Teaching principles such as courtesy, integrity, and self-control can greatly help in these situations, allowing students to navigate issues that may otherwise be challenging to handle.

Conflicts arising from ego can be detrimental in both the dojang and in business settings. Training provides students with an outlet for expressing pent-up emotions and frustrations, which helps prevent conflicts from escalating into confrontations.

Instead, students can direct their energy toward disciplined practice and self-improvement, developing greater resilience to stressful situations. This enables them to manage conflicts effectively, resulting in positive rather than negative outcomes.

Individuals with a background in Taekwondo can foster an environment of open communication, active listening, and a willingness to compromise. This approach facilitates constructive dialogue and helps find mutually beneficial solutions to conflicts.

In a business context, these conflict resolution skills can be extremely valuable.

Mental Health and Well-being:

Teaching the importance of good health and mental mindfulness empowers students with tools for training and success. By practicing meditation and mindfulness, students can quiet their minds, manage stress, and cultivate a sense of inner peace and harmony. Engaging in mindfulness also helps develop stronger coping skills for the challenges that arise in life.

Example: Helps students manage the pressures associated with upcoming Taekwondo gradings or competitions. These events can impose significant mental and physical demands. By improving a student's mental well-being and self-esteem, we can reduce these stresses, ultimately enhancing their performance in both training and on competition day.

Physical Fitness:

Students should be open to learning and applying themselves to improve physically. Over time, instructors will place greater demands on students, which will be both physically and mentally challenging. Training enhances a student's ability to control their technique, balance, timing, coordination of movement, composure, and response to physical stress, among other skills.

Consistent training not only improves a student's health and vitality but also increases their physical strength and endurance. Taekwondo instructors teach and promote healthier lifestyle choices by encouraging students to eat healthy, rest adequately, and stay properly hydrated.

Goal Setting: S.M.A.R.T.

Students must be proficient in the Taekwondo techniques associated with each level. To advance to the next rank, they should learn and master new skills and techniques. Once they have achieved this proficiency, they will be required to demonstrate their abilities during club gradings. Gradings and competitions serve as common goals for all students.

S.M.A.R.T. is a great way to set and manage goals. Remember, all goals should be achievable:

- Specific
- Measurable
- Accurate
- Relevant
- Time-bound

S.M.A.R.T. goals enable students and instructors to track and monitor a student's progress and stay aligned with their training needs. This approach makes it much easier to track outcomes and clarify the roles each person plays in the process. The desired results are determined collaboratively by everyone involved.

S.M.A.R.T. goals are commonly used in business and serve as an invaluable tool for driving results and establishing key performance indicators (KPIs).

Student A aims to achieve a new rank through grading or needs extra training for an upcoming competition within the next three months. This clarification allows instructors to understand the student's needs and work collaboratively with them to reach their established goals.

Business Example: Your Dojang is launching a new product and planning to expand into new markets, while competitors are pursuing similar strategies. As the business leader, gather your team to develop a strategy that will allow you to capitalize on the opportunity to be the first in the marketplace. To achieve this, set S.M.A.R.T. goals to ensure clarity and focus. This will help all key stakeholders understand their roles and responsibilities in this initiative.

Adaptability:

Adaptability is a core attribute of successful business leaders. It allows them to navigate uncertainty, capitalize on new opportunities, and achieve success. Taekwondo training teaches students to be adaptable to change by exposing them to a diverse range of training methodologies and modalities. This approach challenges students to continually improve, evolve, and grow their skills.

Example: The unpredictable nature of sparring in Taekwondo requires students to think on their feet, adjust their strategies, and respond to changing circumstances immediately. By learning to embrace change and the unknown, students develop greater resilience and confidence in their ability to overcome challenges.

In the fast-paced world of business, the ability to adapt to change is invaluable for success.

Business Management:

These principles and teachings directly apply to the business world:

- Leadership
- Teamwork
- Goal setting
- Conflict resolution

Leadership qualities gained through Taekwondo:

- Integrity
- Humility
- Resilience

These qualities are instrumental in guiding teams toward goals and overcoming any challenges along the way.

The teamwork and collaboration essential in Taekwondo foster a culture of trust, respect, and accountability.

Encouraging open communication, supporting one another, and collaborating to solve problems are essential for success.

Businesses can leverage their team members' unique skills, talents, and diverse perspectives to achieve better outcomes.

By establishing clear and concise S.M.A.R.T. goals, businesses can align their efforts and track their progress effectively.

This approach enables informed decision-making, drives sustainable growth, fosters success, and allows for the management and tracking of key performance indicators.

Marketing and Branding:

Effective marketing strategies enable martial arts businesses to establish a unique identity.

Key components of effective martial arts marketing include:

- Digital Marketing
- Social media engagement
- Community outreach programs
- Word-of-mouth referrals

By leveraging online platforms such as websites, social media channels, and email marketing, martial arts businesses can reach a broader audience.

Engaging with the community and forming partnerships helps these businesses build credibility and goodwill among the public.

Strong branding is essential for differentiating martial arts schools and fostering brand loyalty.

Additionally, continuously researching your target audience is crucial for achieving long-term success in any business.

Taekwondo and the Martial Arts Business Industry:

The Taekwondo martial arts industry offers both unique opportunities and challenges. Success in this field requires a blend of business skills, martial arts expertise, and a passion for teaching and helping others.

Starting a Taekwondo school, selling martial arts equipment, and offering merchandise are viable business options. However, businesses in the martial arts industry must navigate various considerations to achieve success.

Considerations when launching a Taekwondo martial arts business include:

- The Dojang (training hall) location
- Target market
- Pricing strategy
- Instructors
- Training Times
- Facilities
- Equipment needs
- Marketing and promotions

Conducting thorough market research and developing a comprehensive business plan can significantly boost the chances of success and long-term sustainability for martial arts business owners. Seeking guidance from industry experts will enhance this process.

In Summary:

The philosophical principles and teachings of Taekwondo:

- Discipline
- Respect
- Perseverance
- Indomitable spirit

Offer students a strong foundation to effectively navigate the challenges of the business world.

By developing and using the following skills

- Leadership
- Teamwork
- Conflict resolution
- Goal setting

Students who become business leaders can enhance their effectiveness, drive organizational performance, and achieve greater success. The marketing and branding strategies employed by the martial arts industry offer valuable lessons. These strategies can help businesses differentiate themselves, attract new customers, and build brand loyalty.

By embracing the pursuit of personal and business excellence, integrity, and continual improvement—principles rooted in the martial arts ethos—individuals and organizations can realize their full potential.

I wish you, the reader, every success on your martial arts journey and in life.

ABOUT JOHN CONNELLY

AUSTRALIA

Master John Connelly stands as a distinguished master instructor from Australia, renowned for his illustrious career in education spanning back to 1997. With over two decades of expertise in instructing, coaching, and teaching martial arts, he has gained recognition as a United States Open International Medalist. Currently, he serves as the Head Instructor at SMAC Tang Soo Do School in Mareeba, Queensland, and also holds the esteemed position of Head Instructor at Sports Martial Arts Combat (SMAC). Master Connelly exemplifies excellence in martial arts leadership, and his inclusion in Elite Martial Artists Worldwide Volume III highlights his exceptional skills and contributions to the field.

FOR MORE INFORMATION:

- SMAC Sports Martial Arts Combat
- Website: www.movingwell.org

CHAPTER EIGHTEEN

COMMUNICATION

BY NICK DONATO

Put simply, communication is "shared or exchanged information, news, or ideas." But today's society has made it anything but that simple!

In business, effective communication can mean the difference between achieving your goals as you envisioned them or merely realizing a diluted version of your original idea. In martial arts, it can determine whether a student successfully overcomes personal challenges or falls victim to misconceptions that are often far removed from reality. In leadership, human communication and connections operate on many levels, including actions, spoken words, tone of voice, and body language. These are just a few tools that people use to convey and receive complete messages. It's important to note that I am not referring to artificial intelligence or technological devices when discussing communication. Each individual is an expert in their smart devices in their own unique way. However, it's essential to remember that complete martial arts is a face-to-face, human-to-human experience—an activity and a personal growth opportunity that is difficult to quantify. The type of communication required and its vital role in each person's journey is crucial.

"Communication works for those who work at it." – John Powell

I am extremely grateful that I did not grow up in an environment dominated by smart devices. I had to be home before the streetlights came on, and no one could call me since we didn't have mobile phones. I had to remember my home phone number and write down the contact numbers of the important people in my life. Besides the occasional quick conversation on the landline phone, which was fixed in a specific spot in the house, all my conversations with others were face to face. These conversations could range from difficult and embarrassing to funny, involving my failures or requests for help. There were no screens to hide behind and no option to send a text. While some might view life back then as outdated, the advantage was that after these conversations, the emotional baggage I had built up in my mind was addressed immediately, allowing me to move on mentally and emotionally. This meant that there was no unnecessary anxiety lingering in my mind—a stark contrast to today's society, where such anxiety seems to accumulate, leading to overwhelming negativity and potentially contributing to depression. I'm not referring to PTSD (Post-Traumatic Stress Disorder), which is a different issue that requires its own form of support through communication. Many people I encounter find it refreshing that I am honest, direct, and prefer face-to-face communication. When I am asked for advice, I often notice that those individuals seem emotionally challenged because honesty and directness only resonate with those seeking the truth—not with those looking for a comforting, gentle response. Nevertheless, deep down, the conscious mind craves the truth to find solutions, even if one may not want to hear it.

"The single biggest problem in communication is the illusion that it has taken place." – George Bernard Shaw

When I teach Tai Chi to students of all ages, I often notice a few students at the back of the class having a private conversation. To redirect their attention back to my lesson, I sometimes tell a fictional story about a goanna that wandered into the back paddock and started attacking the chickens. I describe how the rooster bravely fought to protect them, and I continue the story for as long as needed to regain focus. My long-term students usually grin at this and enjoy hearing the latest version of my "on-the-spot fictional story of distraction." Newer students, however, often ask whether the rooster and the chickens are okay. This illustrates an important point: just because a conversation occurs doesn't guarantee that everyone who needs to hear it has done so, or that they fully understand it.

The most effective communicators are able to determine whether their message, information, or instructions have been received as intended. If they find that the communication was not effective, they look for alternative methods to convey their message. This could involve making the interaction more engaging, changing the format of delivery, or choosing a more appropriate time to communicate. While the current array of communication devices offers convenience and allows for real-time responses, we must consider the potential costs. People often refer to the "feels," which relates to the limbic system—a collection of structures in the brain that regulates emotions, behavior, motivation, and memory. Despite its small size, the limbic system plays a crucial role in how we interact with the world around us. This aspect is something that telemarketers and advertisers often seek to manipulate. The term "feels" is internet slang for "feelings." It signifies an overwhelming emotional reaction, and the phrase "to feel all the feels" means to experience a wide range of strong emotions. This development is fascinating, especially considering it has evolved through a medium that lacks physical sensations such as touch, smell, taste, and, most importantly, our sixth sense. Over generations, society has diminished the significance of the sixth sense, which serves as an innate survival mechanism within all of us. Without regular interaction through conversation, and without the ability to read body language and breath, we risk losing the true essence of understanding where a person—whether a friend, family member, or student—is emotionally.

"When people talk listen completely. Most people never listen."– Ernest Hemingway

Communication extends far beyond simply sharing knowledge. As Martial Arts Instructors, we must take on various roles. Our responsibility goes beyond just teaching kicks and punches; we must also empower and encourage those in front of us. The most crucial starting point in this process is to listen. As I enter my fifth decade in this industry, I have found that listening is the key to effective technical coaching. Decades ago, when I discussed the value of different techniques, I used an analogy of a Mini Moke or a Volkswagen van colliding with a Mack truck. Now, when I teach the same lesson, I reference an electric vehicle (EV) colliding with a truck to convey the same understanding.

"Effective communication is 20% what you know and 80% how you feel about what you know." – Jim Rohn

The development of board-breaking skills is heavily influenced by the 20% / 80% concept. Approaching a board to break it for the first time can stir up a whirlwind of emotions. It's often said that "assumption is the mother of all mistakes." I frequently observe students who have dedicated years to perfecting their technique abandon all their hard work at the moment of execution. For some reason—though it's not really a mystery—fear (which can be described as "false events appearing real") begins to take over, undermining their confidence. However, if students have trained diligently over the years and expressed their thoughts and feelings leading up to this moment, then fear can be reframed to mean "face everything and rise." It's crucial for students to engage in discussions with those who have come before them. Similarly, instructors, leaders, and businesspeople should pay close attention—not only to what is being said but also to what remains unspoken.

The art of communication is, in many ways, a journey. Those who have built successful businesses and martial arts systems over the years will agree that their communication with students, networks, and colleagues in the past is vastly different from their approach today. As human beings, our ability to empathize, along with our perspective and insights gained from life experiences, shape the depth and extent of our conversations. Although we may long for the simplicity of the past, it is impossible to return to those "good old days."

Just like the Zen story: *A martial arts student went to his teacher and said earnestly, "I am devoted to studying your martial system. How long will it take me to master it?"*

The teacher's reply was casual, "Ten years."

Impatiently, the student answered, "But I want to master it faster than that. I will work very hard. I will practice every day, ten or more hours a day if I must. How long will it take then?"

The teacher thought for a moment, "20 years."

-Unknown

The story is somewhat underwhelming, but it highlights an important truth: when we strongly desire something, we can often end up pushing it away. It's essential to maintain a beginner's mind. This mindset allows us to hear and speak more clearly, enabling us to draw on the insights of others in order to reach our business goals, achieve personal targets, and help students overcome obstacles that can be life-changing. Ultimately, our aim in all our endeavors should be to make a difference in the world, share our learning experiences and knowledge with those who seek assistance, and find purpose in each day. However, none of this is possible without effective communication. As we journey through life, we come to realize that consistent communication and the loyalty it fosters are fundamental to creating, developing, and maintaining everything we invest our heart and soul into, both emotionally and physically.

If people paid as much attention to the communication happening around them in the present moment—specifically to the individuals they are sharing space with—mental health would not be the minefield it is today. Facebook refers to random strangers as "friends," which is an informal use of the term. The correct definition of a friend is "a person with whom one has a bond of mutual affection." If we have a distorted sense of our relationships, how can our conversations support the relationships, business ventures, leadership directions, and other goals we aspire to achieve? Understanding the characters and the roles they play in our lives is crucial. Only by doing so can we tailor the depth of our communication to fit the narrative, purpose, or need at hand. Some people come into your life for only a season; these are known as "leaf people." They take what they want and move on when the winds of change come. Then there are those who may stick around through certain seasons but leave when things get tough. While they may seem resilient, they struggle with the difficult aspects of life; we can think of these as "branch people." Recognizing and identifying these different characters allows you to adjust your communication style to meet both your needs and their goals. However, the most important individuals are those who do not act for the sake of being seen. They support you during challenging times, may not always agree with you, but choose to remain by your side. These are your true friends— the foundation of solid relationships in business, training, life, and love.

Identify these individuals and pursue your path with confidence. Without effective communication, all of this becomes impossible, leaving you stranded in a wilderness of uncertainty, unable to turn your dreams into reality.

If you put yourself out there, say hello, and genuinely cultivate curiosity about the world around you—your family, the community you share your space with, the places you visit, and the industry you dedicate your time and effort to—communication will naturally occur. It truly is an art! I am incredibly grateful for my experiences, as they have allowed me to teach and meet amazing people from all walks of life around the globe. Thanks to effective communication, I have been able to make the most of the opportunities that have come my way. In 2024, I achieved something I never thought possible: I shared the life lessons I've learned and my journey so far in my international bestselling book, "The Memoirs of Master Nick Donato – My Journey as an Aussie Martial Artist."

So, remember: *"Honest, open communication is the only street that leads us into the real world... We then begin to grow as never before. And once we are on this road, happiness cannot be far away."* — John Joseph Powel

ABOUT NICK DONATO

AUSTRALIA

Master Nick Donato was born in the southern suburbs of Sydney, Australia. For most of his early years, he was raised by his maternal grandparents while his mother worked multiple jobs to support the family. Nick was especially close to his grandfather, whom he considered his best mate. After his grandfather's sudden death, Nick fell into a deep state of grief and anger, which led him down a troubling path. However, martial arts provided him with the focus and clarity he needed to slowly overcome his struggles and regain control of his life.

Master Nick's perspective on life transformed over his 55-plus years in the martial arts industry. This journey has become not only his calling but also his education. Today, he is a highly sought-after teacher, eager to share the power of martial arts with the world. Nick is a father of two, a grandfather of four, and a guiding father figure to hundreds of people of all ages. His path has been filled with many challenges and crossroads, but his mindset of "using no way as a way," along with his love for martial arts, has led him to a peaceful and fulfilling place in life.

FOR MORE INFORMATION:

- Personal Defence Studios Pty Ltd - The PIT Martial Arts Health & Fitness
- Websites: www.thepitmartialarts.com/au, www.kwonbopdofederation.com, www.masternickdonato.com
- Facebook: @thepitmartialarts, @nickdonato
- Instagram: @pdsmartialarts

CHAPTER NINETEEN

KEVIN HOOKER'S JOURNEY IN MARTIAL ARTS & BUSINESS

BY KEVIN HOOKER

Introduction:

Every martial artist knows that dedication, discipline, and perseverance are the cornerstones of success in the dojo. However, not every martial artist understands that the same qualities are essential to succeeding in business. My journey from a college student studying Shotokan Karate to the owner of a successful martial arts dojo has been a path of continuous learning, both on the mat and in the world of business. In this chapter, I will share insights on how martial arts principles translated into business success, the challenges I encountered along the way, and the lessons I learned that can help others build a strong foundation for their martial arts careers.

Starting Out: The Power of Opportunity

I began my martial arts journey in college at the University of Nebraska-Lincoln under the guidance of Professor Richard Schmidt, who introduced me to Shotokan Karate. My passion for martial arts grew alongside my involvement in cheerleading, and I soon found myself teaching gymnastics to incoming athletes. This was the first glimpse I had into the world of teaching and mentoring, but it also laid the groundwork for my business ventures.

As a college student, I was fortunate to have access to the gymnastic facilities at Nebraska-Lincoln and a network of athletes and coaches. This network proved invaluable when I transitioned into teaching gymnastics and tumbling. One of my closest friends, a gymnast, had an injury that forced him to shift his focus from competing to teaching, and this is where our journey as entrepreneurs truly began.

We started by working with small groups of athletes, offering private lessons and charging a modest fee. What began as a way to help athletes improve their skills turned into a business. We quickly realized that there was a demand for what we were offering, and soon, our schedule was booked for hours with clients eager to learn. This experience taught me the value of seizing opportunities when they arise, no matter how small they might seem at first.

The initial success was a turning point, and it instilled in me the mindset that anything is possible when you take action and provide value. From a simple notebook tracking lessons and payments, we were able to scale our business and teach dozens of athletes every week. The entrepreneurial spirit that was sparked in those early days carried me forward and laid the foundation for my career in martial arts.

Transitioning to Kenpo Karate and Opening My Dojo

After graduation, I moved to Omaha, which was about an hour away from Nebraska-Lincoln. As much as I wanted to continue my Shotokan training, commuting back and forth wasn't feasible, so I found a new dojo in Omaha that focused on Kenpo Karate. Little did I know that this new martial art would become a major part of my life. Over the next 26 years, Kenpo became my focus, and I honed my skills in the art, ultimately leading me to open my own dojo in 2008.

At the time, I was content as a student, but something within me kept urging me to take the next step and open a dojo. I began to question why I was holding myself back, and ultimately, the drive to share my passion for martial arts with others pushed me to make the leap into business.

Opening a dojo was both exciting and challenging. Initially, I wasn't interested in being a business owner, but I couldn't pass up the opportunity to teach and mentor others in the martial arts community. The dojo became my "baby," and I poured all my energy into making it successful.

The Importance of a No-Quit Mentality

One of the most important lessons I've learned throughout my martial arts and business journey is the power of persistence and resilience. Failure was never an option in my mind, and that mentality kept me going through the toughest times. Like many new businesses, the dojo faced its fair share of setbacks. There were times when the bills piled up, and I struggled to keep the doors open. But through sheer determination, I kept pushing forward.

There were plenty of obstacles to overcome—financial difficulties, unexpected expenses, and even moments of self-doubt. But I learned that success is about what you do when things don't go according to plan. Instead of blaming external circumstances or other people, I chose to look internally for ways to improve. Taking responsibility for my decisions and actions allowed me to learn and grow from each mistake.

The key to success in business, much like in martial arts, is never to give up. In the dojo, if you fall, you get back up. When faced with challenges in business, you find a way to adapt and keep moving forward. This mentality of "no quit" has helped me and countless others achieve success in martial arts and beyond.

Building the Business: Taking Accountability and Bending Reality to Your Will

As I continued to develop my business, I learned that being a successful business owner requires taking 100% accountability for everything that happens within your company. From financial decisions to customer satisfaction, every part of your business is a direct result of your actions.

When I first started, I had no idea how to handle budgets, taxes, and the many administrative tasks of running a dojo. There were times when I had to rob Peter to pay Paul—sacrificing personal expenses to ensure the business could survive. But these early struggles taught me how to budget, prioritize, and make critical decisions.

I also learned that running a business isn't just about working hard—it's about working smart. Sometimes, I would spend hours on tasks that didn't move the needle forward for the dojo. With the right mentorship, I learned how to delegate and focus on the high-impact activities that would grow the business. Being strategic with my time and resources allowed me to maximize the dojo's potential.

The Role of Mentorship in Business

I had no idea what I was doing in my early days as a business owner. Like many young entrepreneurs, I was stubborn and wanted to prove I could succeed. However, I quickly realized that I didn't have all the answers. Mentorship played a crucial role in my development as a business owner.

I was fortunate to have mentors who guided me through the ups and downs of entrepreneurship. These mentors provided invaluable insights into everything from marketing to customer retention. They helped me navigate the challenges of running a business and gave me the tools I needed to succeed.

One of the most important things I learned from my mentors was the importance of asking for help. In my twenties, I didn't want to admit that I didn't know something, but asking for guidance and learning from others who had been there before was one of the best decisions I could have made. A good mentor doesn't just give you answers—they ask the right questions to help you discover solutions on your own.

The Business of Martial Arts: Marketing and Branding

One of the biggest challenges I faced was understanding the business side of martial arts. Many martial artists start schools with the belief that if you open a dojo, people will come. But that's simply not true. The reality is that a successful martial arts school requires more than just great instruction; it requires effective marketing and branding.

Building a strong brand and marketing your dojo is essential to attracting new students and retaining existing ones. In my early years, I struggled with marketing, but over time, I learned the importance of creating a recognizable brand and consistently promoting it. This meant creating a clear message about what my dojo stood for and how it could benefit students.

Marketing is about more than just advertising; it's about building relationships with potential students and the community. In martial arts, people are seeking more than just a place to learn self-defense—they are looking for a place where they can grow as individuals, develop discipline, and build confidence. Your marketing should reflect that.

Giving Back: The Key to Long-Term Success

Throughout my journey, I've learned that the most successful businesses are those that focus on giving back to others. Martial arts is about personal growth, but it's also about sharing your knowledge and helping others achieve their goals. This mindset has been instrumental in the success of my dojo.

When you focus on helping others, your own success will follow. This doesn't mean ignoring your own needs or goals but rather recognizing that when you help others succeed, you create a community of people who will support and elevate you in return. Whether it's through teaching martial arts or offering mentorship, giving back is a core principle that has guided my business practices.

Conclusion: Lessons Learned and Moving Forward

In conclusion, my journey from a college student practicing Shotokan Karate to finding the system of Kenpo Karate to being the owner of a successful dojo has been filled with valuable lessons. Business success, much like in martial arts, is about perseverance, continuous learning, and never giving up. The challenges I faced along the way have shaped me into the business owner I am today.

I hope my story serves as inspiration for others who are considering a career in martial arts and business. By embracing a no-quit mentality, taking accountability for your actions, and focusing on the needs of others, you can build a successful martial arts school that will thrive for years to come.

ABOUT KEVIN HOOKER

USA

Shihan Kevin started his martial arts journey in 1991 in Shotokan Karate at the University of Nebraska-Lincoln under Professor Richard Schmidt. After graduating with an engineering degree and moving to Omaha, he found a new home in Kenpo Karate. Kevin is now the chief instructor for the martial arts program at the Elite Academy of Martial Arts, beginning Kenpo training under Shihan Tom Scott in 1999. After achieving his black belt, Shihan Kevin enrolled in the Sensei Program to apply his love of teaching to his love of martial arts.

After apprenticing under Shihan Scott in the proper way to share NCK, Kevin Hooker earned his Sensei title from Shihan Scott. With Shihan Scott retiring from the commercial school in 2010, he was given the opportunity to continue Shihan Scott's mission to maintain a prestige-level kenpo karate school in the mid-west.

Kevin is currently a 6th-degree black belt (Rokudan) in Kenpo Karate and continues to strive to perfect his skills in martial arts, now training under Professor Nick Chamberlain Judan (10th degree) out of Dallas, TX. In the spirit of continuing to strive for more - Kevin took up Brazilian JiuJitsu under Fabio Santos's/Rickson Gracie black belt Greg James, where Kevin attained the rank of black belt in the Summer of 2023. In 2022, Shihan Kevin was honored and humbled to be part of a collaboration to co-author a book, *Elite Martial Artists in America: Secrets to Life, Leadership & Business, Volumes I & II* (released in January 2023 and February of 2024).

Today, Shihan Kevin continues teaching and is working on several new concepts, including starting a podcast and creating a new martial arts system to grow even more within the community.

FOR MORE INFORMATION:

- Elite Academy of Martial Arts
- Email: kevin@karateofomaha.com

CHAPTER TWENTY

BUILDING A BUSINESS FROM THE GROUND UP

BY MAGGIE MESSINA

In embarking on the journey of establishing a business from scratch, I discovered the significance of identifying that single passion that drives and motivates me. Once I discovered this passion, I committed myself to pursuing it, consistently keeping it at the forefront of my efforts. For me, failure has never been an option.

There are several key principles to keep in mind:

(1) **Organization is Crucial:** Maintaining organization is vital. It is essential to keep your mission clear and prominent. Never lose sight of your original purpose, regardless of the distractions or temptations that may arise.

(2) **Staffing Matters:** Appropriate staffing is essential for success. The saying "one bad apple can spoil the bunch" is particularly relevant in the business environment. From my own experiences, I have learned that negativity can be detrimental to team dynamics. If you have a staff member who constantly complains—whether about their workload or the team's performance—this negativity can undermine the morale of the entire team. Such individuals, often labeled as "the black cloud," should be addressed and, if necessary, removed promptly.

③ **Stay Present:** In the martial arts industry, it is crucial for leaders to remain engaged. As business founders become busier, they may tend to step back and delegate tasks but staying involved is essential. Continuous personal and professional development is key; never assume you have all the answers. Seek out new knowledge and be open to learning from anyone, regardless of their background or experience.

④ **Embrace Diversity in Education:** Throughout my years of teaching and managing my business, I have observed that a teacher's effectiveness is not determined by gender. What truly matters is the content and delivery of the material. Today, the landscape is evolving, and women in martial arts can provide just as much value, if not more, than their male counterparts. It is essential to recognize that the value of instruction lies in the knowledge shared, rather than the identity of the instructor.

⑤ **Personal Growth is Fundamental:** People often ask me about the greatest challenges I face in business. I have realized that my biggest challenge is often myself. Through exercise, diet, and therapy, I have learned the importance of self-improvement. By addressing my own issues and working through my challenges, I become a better teacher, mentor, and entrepreneur. Without ongoing self-improvement, we cannot hope to grow.

As I reflect on my journey, I realize that resilience is equally important. The path to starting a business is often filled with challenges and setbacks. However, it is essential to view these obstacles as opportunities for growth rather than as hindrances. Each challenge we encounter offers a valuable lesson, and these experiences ultimately help shape a stronger and more adaptable leader.

⑥ **Networking is Key:** Building a network of contacts can significantly impact your business success. Surround yourself with like-minded individuals who share your vision and values. Collaborate with others in your field, attend workshops, and engage in community events. These connections can provide invaluable support, resources, and insights that can help you navigate the complexities of entrepreneurship.

⑦ **Adaptability is Vital:** The business landscape is constantly evolving, and being adaptable is crucial for survival. Embrace change and be willing to pivot your strategies when necessary. Stay informed about market trends, consumer preferences, and technological advancements. A flexible approach enables you to seize new opportunities and remain competitive.

⑧ **Customer Focus is Essential:** Your business ultimately exists to serve your customers. Prioritize their needs and feedback to create an exceptional experience. Building strong relationships with clients fosters loyalty and encourages referrals, which can be instrumental in your business growth. Always listen to and learn from their insights, as these can guide you in refining your offerings.

⑨ **Celebrate Small Wins:** In the pursuit of larger goals, it's easy to overlook smaller milestones. Make it a point to celebrate these achievements, no matter how minor they may seem. Recognizing your progress not only boosts morale but also reinforces the idea that you are moving in the right direction. These celebrations can foster a positive atmosphere within your team and remind everyone of the collective effort involved in the journey.

⑩ **Balance is Important:** Finally, while it is essential to be dedicated to your business, it is equally important to maintain a balance between work and personal life for long-term sustainability. Prioritize self-care and carve out time for family, friends, and hobbies. Leading a well-rounded life enhances your overall well-being, which in turn fuels your passion and creativity in your business pursuits.

Improving time management skills can significantly enhance productivity and reduce stress. Here are some effective strategies to consider:

① **Set Clear Goals:** Define short-term and long-term goals. Use the SMART criteria—Specific, Measurable, Achievable, Relevant, and Time-bound—to ensure your goals are clear and attainable.

② **Prioritize Tasks:** Identify the most important tasks utilizing methods like the Eisenhower Matrix, which categorizes tasks into four quadrants based on their urgency and importance. Focus on high-priority tasks first.

③ **Create a Daily Schedule:** Plan your day by allocating specific time blocks for different tasks. Use tools like calendars or planners to visualize your schedule and stick to it as closely as possible.

④ **Use Time Blocking:** Dedicate specific blocks of time to focus solely on tasks or projects. This approach helps reduce distractions and increases concentration.

⑤ **Set Deadlines:** Even for tasks without strict deadlines, setting your own can create a sense of urgency and help you stay on track.

⑥ **Limit Distractions:** Identify common distractions and find ways to minimize them. This could involve turning off notifications, creating a dedicated workspace, or using apps that block distracting websites.

⑦ **Take Breaks:** Incorporate short breaks into your schedule to recharge. Techniques like the Pomodoro Technique - 25 minutes of focused work followed by a 5-minute break - can enhance focus and productivity.

⑧ **Review and Reflect:** At the end of each week, take time to review what you accomplished. Reflect on what worked well and what didn't and adjust your strategies accordingly.

⑨ **Learn to Say No:** Be mindful of your limits and avoid overcommitting. Saying no to tasks or projects that don't align with your goals can free up time for what truly matters.

⑩ **Utilize Technology:** Leverage apps and tools designed for time management, such as task managers, calendars, and timers. These can help you organize tasks and keep track of your time effectively.

⑪ **Delegate When Possible:** If you're part of a team, don't hesitate to delegate tasks that others can manage. This allows you to concentrate on your strengths and priorities.

⑫ **Establish Routines:** Create daily routines that align with your peak productivity times. Consistency in these routines can help you develop good habits and optimize your workflow.

By implementing these strategies, you can enhance your time management skills, leading to increased efficiency and a more balanced life.

In summary, the path of entrepreneurship is not a straight line; it is a winding road filled with lessons, growth, and opportunities. By staying organized, fostering a supportive team, remaining engaged, and continuously improving yourself, you set a solid foundation for success. Embrace your fears, take calculated risks, and remember

that your passion, combined with knowledge and experience, will guide you to achieve your dreams.
Your journey is uniquely yours, and by honoring that journey, you will find fulfillment and success in ways you may not have previously imagined.

Knowledge and experience are powerful allies on the path to success. Embrace your journey and the lessons that come with it. Remember, failure is only a viable option if you choose to make it one.

Stay true, stay YOU!

ABOUT MAGGIE MESSINA

USA

Bio/CV:

- Maggie is one of the first generation of women to own and operate a martial arts school. Master Maggie founded Taecole in 1996, and it has been continuously operating since then.
- Maggie is a highly skilled martial artist who has won multiple gold medals representing the USA.
- Maggie was a project coordinator for many years at Sloan Kettering Cancer Center in New York City. Each year, she organizes several drives for toys, clothing, and food, personally delivering the items to women and children in homeless shelters.
- Maggie has received many awards and accolades throughout her career, including but not limited to:
    o The Presidential Lifetime Achievement Award
    o The Most Powerful Woman in Business for NYS (Schneps Media)

- o The New York Assembly Certificate of Merit for Female Fighters Matter Too (Founder and President)
  - o The Martial Artist Legacy Award (AMAA).
- She also has received Special Congressional Recognition for her "outstanding and invaluable service to her community and everywhere she makes her mark," and Special Recognition by NYS Senator Joseph P. Adabbo, Jr. for her "selflessness and tireless commitment to the State of New York and her loyalty and dedication to the betterment of the State of New York."

FOR MORE INFORMATION:

- Taecole Tae Kwon Do and Fitness/Female Fighters Matter Too Inc.
- Website: www.taecoletkd.com
- Email: maggiemessina@icloud.com
- Instagram: @taecoletkdkarate

CHAPTER TWENTY-ONE

THE JOY OF LIVING BUSINESS: VISUALIZE & WIN

BY NATHAN RAY

Business in the New Age

Let's begin this journey with a simple yet powerful concept: goal.

A goal starts as a thought—an idea, a spark, a flash of light in the darkness. But how does one become the greatest version of oneself in business? This question is both profound and extraordinarily simple. And because it is so simple, it is often overlooked in favor of more enticing distractions—the shiny objects that pull us in different directions.

Before we can move forward, we must begin with a *proper assessment* of where we are and who we are at this moment. Take an honest and open look at yourself. Reflect deeply. But don't stay there too long—that's a trap. Instead, move forward by making a real decision about what you truly want.

One of my great mentors, Bob Proctor, often said: *"You only get one bite at the apple."*

That statement resonated deeply with me, stirring my emotions and pushing me to reflect. It awakened something inside me—a vision of my greater self and who I could *become*. And now, I ask you to do the same.

Go to the *core* of who you are. Be brutally honest with yourself. Decide where you're going. Decide what you truly want in this life. Now, let's make it simple.

Two Steps to Success in Business and Life

① Determine where you are right now.

② Determine who you want to become.

That's it.

What do you want your life and business to look like? How do you want to live? The truth is, you can live any way you *decide* to. But here's the problem—most people don't know how to *tap into* their own potential. I know because I was once in that same position. I chased success, wealth, and greatness for years. And while my drive led me in the right direction—toward the right people, books, and ideas— I missed one *critical* component.

The Missing Piece

Like most people, I was trained to believe that collecting knowledge and regurgitating it would lead to success. Get a diploma, a degree, or a certification, and you'll get results. That's a lie.

Why am I happy about this? Because if you're reading this, you're questioning the same thing. And that means your awareness is already expanding. You're beginning to think differently.

This is where true change begins.

Understanding the Mind

In school, we learn to *collect* knowledge. But we are not taught *how to use it*. Reading and writing are powerful tools, but unless we absorb them at a deeper level, they remain just that—tools left unused.

Let's break this down with a simple model:

Imagine a **large circle** divided in half by a horizontal line. The **top half** represents your *conscious mind*—your thinking, analytical mind. The **bottom half** represents your *subconscious mind*—the deeper part of you that controls your habits, emotions, and automatic behaviors.

Below that, imagine a **small circle** representing your *body*.

This model helps explain why most people struggle to change. We take in knowledge consciously, but unless it *sinks* into the subconscious mind, nothing changes.

How Do You Reprogram the Subconscious Mind?

The answer is simple: **spaced repetition**.

This was my mistake. I was reading all the right books, listening to the right audio, and attending the right seminars—but I was treating them like checkboxes. I would read something once, feel like I had learned it, and then move on. I was missing the real key: repetition.

Enjoy Living Business Edition: Visualize and Win

Let me say a few more words about visualization in business.

Our **self-image** is vital. It is the image we hold of ourselves that will either attract or repel others. You've heard people say someone has a *magnetic personality*. What creates that magnetism?

One major factor is **attitude**. Having the right, positive attitude attracts like-minded people. It also fuels **enthusiasm**—and enthusiasm is contagious. When you are truly energized about something, others match your energy.

But here's an important key: **don't just visualize yourself**.

Yes, you must develop a strong self-image, and if you don't have one, the good news is that you can change it *at any moment*. However, in business, you must also help **others** see the greatness within themselves.

The Secret to Business Success: Service to Others

Here's the secret: serve others first, and you will have everything you need. Building a successful business is about relationships.

Napoleon Hill, in *Think and Grow Rich*, emphasized the importance of going the **extra mile** when serving others. Going beyond what is expected—delivering service at an unmatched level—will place you in a category all your own.

People say, *"It's the little things that mean a lot."* That is not just a cliché—it is a **universal law**. Treat your customers like they are the most important people in the world—because, to them, they are.

The **giants of business** are the greatest servants. They serve **more people** and deliver **more value**, and in return, they receive **greater rewards**—many times over. Earl Nightingale, in *The Strangest Secret*, described a man sitting in front of a fireplace demanding heat, yet refusing to put in the firewood. This is how many people approach business. They want results without first making the investment.

But that's not how universal law works. The **law of cause and effect** is absolute. You must **give first**—and give generously. When you put in small effort, you get small results. But if you give *greatly*, the rewards will be just as great.

The Key Differentiator in Business

If you want to stand out in your field, it won't be because of your **product alone**—others are offering something similar.

Your true differentiators are:

- **Your attitude**
- **Your enthusiasm**
- **Your level of service to others**

Master these, and you will become a leader in your industry.

Final Thoughts

This is just the beginning. In my *Joy of Living* series, I go deeper into these concepts, but for now, understand this: Your business success is simple. It all comes down to:

① **Clarifying your goals**

② **Reprogramming your paradigm through repetition**

③ **Using visualization to solidify your success**

④ **Serving others at the highest level**

Until you break the old paradigm and install a new one, your results will remain the same.

The great masters who taught these principles may have passed on, but their wisdom remains. Their books and teachings still exist. But most importantly, there must be *living voices*—people who can continue spreading these truths and guiding others to their next level of success. I am one of those voices.

Let's connect, communicate, and build something greater together. Your success is within reach. All you have to do is claim it.

ABOUT NATHAN RAY

USA

Bushi Tensei Nathan Ray is a 10th Degree Black Belt, an international best-selling author, a certified international speaker, a model, and an award-winning actor. He is also the recent recipient of the Grandmaster of the Year award from the Action Martial Arts Hall of Honors. His karate dojo, World Karate Do, was recently named one of the top 20 schools in the world by the American Martial Arts Alliance.

In his latest work, The Joy of Living: Business Edition, Bushi Tensei Nathan Ray explores the power of visualization, self-image, and paradigm shifts in business success. This chapter, Visualize and Win, dives into the universal laws of cause and effect, the magnetic force of attitude, and the importance of serving others at the highest level. Drawing wisdom from mentors such as Bob Proctor, Napoleon Hill, and Earl Nightingale, he illustrates how business success is not a matter of luck, but of deliberate thought, action, and repetition of the right ideas. His message is clear: shift your paradigm, serve with excellence, and watch success follow.

FOR MORE INFORMATION:

- World Karate Do, Knightdale, NC
- Website: www.worldkaratedoknightdale.com
- Email: n.ray@mac.com
- Facebook: www.facebook.com/share/18SmnknRYc/?
- YouTube: @themasterycenter371

www.ingramcontent.com/pod-product-compliance
Lightning Source LLC
Chambersburg PA
CBHW070623100426
42744CB00006B/592